Astrology's Zodiac Archetypes

What People Are Saying About

Astrology's Zodiac Archetypes

Astrology's roots are deeply entwined with ancient metaphysics. Somehow that connection got broken. I can only thank Bernie Ashman and Carmen Turner-Schott for helping us heal those broken bones, reminding us that true astrology is ultimately about the care of the soul in its long homeward journey.
Steven Forrest, bestselling author of *The Inner Sky*

This is a timeless, rich and exciting book. Bernie Ashman and Carmen Turner-Schott have come together to bring to light our unique Zodiac Archetypes. As master astrologers they reveal our archetypical strengths and challenges with clarity and precision. Exploring our relationship with the skies in this easy-to-read guide is a blueprint for transformation, healing and living a happier and more satisfying life.
Sherrie Dillard, bestselling author of *I'm Still with You, Heal and Evolve with Your Loved One on the Other Side*, and *You Are Psychic*

Carmen and Bernie are my two favorite astrologers. They write in a practical way that makes astrology understandable on a psychological level. As a psychology professor, I have been interested in how astrology, psychology, and archetypes are connected. In this book, the authors deep-dive into past life patterns and help the reader tap into their strengths to heal. I love this book and highly recommend it to anyone who wants to learn more about themselves and others.
Sherianna Boyle, bestselling author of *Just Ask Spirt* and the *Emotional Detox Series*

What People Are Saying About Astrology's Zodiac Archetypes

Astrology's Zodiac Archetypes

Bernie Ashman and
Carmen Turner-Schott

BOOKS

London, UK
Washington, DC, USA

CollectiveInk

First published by O-Books, 2026
O-Books is an imprint of Collective Ink Ltd.,
Unit 11, Shepperton House, 89 Shepperton Road, London, N1 3DF
office@collectiveinkbooks.com
www.collectiveinkbooks.com
www.o-books.com

For distributor details and how to order, please visit the 'Ordering' section on our website.

Text copyright: Bernie Ashman and Carmen Turner-Schott, 2025

ISBN: 978 1 917704 32 8
978 1 917704 68 7 (ebook)
Library of Congress Control Number: 2025937557

A CIP catalogue record for this book is available from the British Library.

Design: Lapiz Digital Services

UK: Printed and bound by CPI Group (UK) Ltd, Croydon, CR0 4YY
Printed in North America by CPI GPS partners

The authors of this book do not dispense medical advice or prescribe the use of any technique as a form of treatment for physical, emotional, or medical problems without the advice of a physician, either directly or indirectly. The intent of the authors is only to offer information of a general nature to help you in your quest for emotional and spiritual well-being. In the event you use any of the information in this book for yourself, which is your constitutional right, the authors and the publisher assume no responsibility for your actions.

The manufacturer's authorised representative in the EU for product safety is:
eucomply OÜ - Pärnu mnt 139b-14, 11317 Tallinn, Estonia,
hello@ eucompliancepartner.com, www.eucompliancepartner.com

We operate a distinctive and ethical publishing philosophy in all areas of our business, from our global network of authors to production and worldwide distribution.

Table of Contents

About the Authors

Carmen Turner-Schott, MSW, LCSW is a bestselling author of 11 books. *The Mysteries of the Twelfth Astrological House: Fallen Angels; Astrology's Magical Nodes of the Moon;* and *Phoenixes and Angels: Mastering the Eighth & Twelfth Astrological Houses* are her most popular books. For the past 30 years she has worked as a trauma therapist, licensed clinical social worker, psychological astrologer, and teacher with national and international clientele. She completed her Master of Social Work degree at Washington University in St Louis, Missouri in 1999. Carmen began her astrological work aged 16 after an experience with a glowing ball of light in her doorway and began studying religion, metaphysics and the Edgar Cayce teachings. She has presented astrology workshops for Kepler College of Astrology, and the Association of Research and Enlightenment (A.R.E.) throughout the years and teaches a variety of spiritual development classes. She is the founder of Deep Soul Divers Astrology and is the creator of several Facebook astrology groups with over 50,000 members. Visit her website at www. carmenturnerschott.com.

Bernie Ashman is the author of several astrology books. He has written two bestselling past life books, and many consider his most popular book, *How to Survive Mercury*, to be the best book written on Mercury retrograde cycles. Bernie is a professional astrologer serving clients internationally. His insightful interpretations have also been utilized for astrology software programs used worldwide and are now produced by Cosmic Patterns in the US. He lives in Durham, NC. Visit his website at www.bernieashman.com.

About the Artist

Michelle Stapleford was born in Nottingham, England, in 1966. She is a self-taught portrait, seascape, and landscape artist, working in oils, watercolors, graphite, and pastels. Her mother encouraged her love of art at a young age. After retiring, Michelle moved to rural Wales and enrolled in the Gwbert School of Art. She studied various artistic techniques under the guidance of artist and illustrator, Rebecca de Winter. Michelle has exhibited her work at Picton Castle Gallery in Pembrokeshire and King Street Gallery in Carmarthen, Wales. Her seascape painting won the best painting in a competition. Michelle started studying astrology in 2012 and has been a member of Carmen Turner Schott's Facebook astrology groups for over ten years. Follow her Facebook Page at https://m. facebook.com/ArtistMichelleStapleford.

Introduction

Archetypes and Psychology

Carmen's Perspective

When I was in college, I especially enjoyed taking psychology classes. Learning about different theories of personality was inspiring and reminded me of my love for astrology. I started studying astrology when I was 16 and learning the basic symbols was the key to truly understanding how to interpret birth reports. Each sign, planet, and house have a specific energy that I could connect to. For instance, I am a Virgo, and the imagery and personality traits of Virgo, such as being shy, efficient, detail-oriented, service-oriented, resonated with me.

Astrology became my passion and because of my interest in psychology and its influence on personality that made astrology even more fascinating, I decided to major in psychology. I wanted to help people on a deeper level. I realized that in a short astrology session people would share that they felt like the sessions helped them more than twelve sessions of traditional therapy. I saw how powerful astrology counseling could be in helping us understand ourselves and others.

My favorite psychologist has always been Carl Jung. I appreciated how he associated unique personality traits with what he called archetypes. He was also open-minded to the power of astrology, symbols, and dream interpretation. His theory of the collective unconscious made sense to me on a personal level. He believed that we are all connected spiritually and that there were universal symbols that had similar meanings. Jung theorized that there were twelve main archetypes that he believed represented and influenced personality. He also felt that we can experience all twelve archetypes in different ways.

When we dig a little deeper into the Jungian archetypes, we can see that these symbols have a similar meaning to the zodiac signs. Archetypes and astrology are symbolic languages that are used as a tool for developing our sixth sense and intuition. Just as Jung theorized, the symbols in astrology and traits associated with the planets, signs, and houses, make astrology a powerful tool of self-awareness. Just as Carl Jung knew dream symbols were a way for the unconscious mind to communicate through symbols, astrology is also energy and operates in a similar way.

Both tools can offer insights and a deeper awareness about the world we live in. The planets, signs, and houses in astrology are guideposts used to understand deeper parts of ourselves and the connection we have to the world around us. This powerful symbolism allows astrology to be an incredibly transformative tool for growth, healing, and resilience.

Jung's twelve main archetypes are below:

The Hero (Warrior, Crusader, Soldier)
The Regular Person (Realist, Solid Citizen)
The Jester (Comedian)
The Caregiver (Parent, Helper, Supporter)
The Artist (Creator, Inventor)
The Sage (Expert, Planner)
The Lover (Partner, Intimate)
The Magician (Healer, Visionary)
The Explorer (Seeker, Wanderer)
The Ruler (Leader, Boss, Politician)
The Rebel (Outlaw, Revolutionary, Misfit)
The Innocent (Dreamer)

In many traditions, the number twelve is significant. In numerology, the number twelve is a master number, and the energy is associated with completeness, spiritual growth, and divine balance. It represents a full year, twelve months, and the twelve-year cycle. The importance of a twelve-year cycle is that it's often a time when our soul experiences great rebirth. The number twelve also has a spiritual meaning as found in the Bible. There were twelve sons of Jacob which are often associated with the personality traits of each zodiac sign. Jesus selected twelve disciples, and each had their own unique personality traits that influenced history. The twelve astrological signs of the zodiac and their specific personality traits relate to the twelve archetypes that Carl Jung theorized. The energies are the same and resonate through history, religion, and art.

In this book, we are going to connect each Jungian archetype with each of the twelve zodiac signs. We are also going to share how each of the zodiac signs tap into their sixth sense. There will be a discussion on how past life karmic patterns can be recognized and overcome. Tips are shared for each zodiac sign to help the reader change troublesome past life patterns and transform them once and for all.

There are many opinions out there concerning which astrological sign is associated with each archetype. We are going to make it simple and feel that by looking at the sign's key personality traits, energies, and strengths, we can narrow down the most relevant archetype that resonates with each zodiac sign. We can also learn to release "old archetypes" from past lifetimes that are no longer useful in our current life.

Just as astrologers believe that astrology is a map of the soul, Jung believed that archetype symbols were tools that can be used for psychological growth and self-realization.

Karmic Patterns

Bernie's Perspective

This is a book that will guide you to more readily integrate past life karmic relationship energies into your current life. Each of us comes into this life with memories from past lifetimes which are often hidden on an unconscious level. As we proceed on our journey, various life encounters activate these memories. It is true that we can make use of past life talents. We may have a past life memory bank full of positive skills we learned in past lives that can be tapped into. These memories can aid us in maintaining balanced relationships in this incarnation. There are also some past life themes that can impede our growth and paths to greater fulfillment.

A major focus in this book will be to identify those past life relating patterns that correspond to each astrological sign. Understanding these energies can help you tap into hidden talents that already exist within you. The Sun sign and archetype chapters in this book will offer the keys to a roadmap that can help unlock the paths to move beyond the pull of past life energy patterns.

It is a misconception, in my experience as an astrologer, to think of the zodiac sign that you were born into as giving you traits only developed in this life. There is an excellent chance you have past life instincts and abilities that have carried over into this lifetime.

It is the karmic patterns that find us repeating behaviors that keep us stuck in limiting situations that we need to channel into more productive expressions. I think of these karmic patterns as energies that reside in the shadow part of our consciousness that need to be brought out into clearer light. Each of us has some of these karmic shadows following us into this life. Think of this as unfinished business for this incarnation that we can learn to master.

Much of my astrological counseling over the years has been helping people navigate through karmic patterns. Many of these karmic tendencies are linked to past life relationships. What is interesting is that some people don't know a karmic pattern was supposed to already be over in this life. Why do we stay repeating old, worn-out past life behaviors? The answer is that there can be an attachment to these shadowy influences because we get used to acting them out. It is as though they know our name and feel free to come calling. They can take on a life of their own. We do have the freedom to opt out of negative thoughts and actions, but we must acknowledge these shadow energies can exist in us. It is at this time that we can begin to find the inner strength and clarity to walk away from old energy and karmic patterns. It might take some will power and positive reinforcement, but we can divorce ourselves from these past patterns of thinking and stop replaying the past.

Past Lives and Reincarnation

Past lives can reveal themselves through astrology. Edgar Cayce, the famous "sleeping prophet", did hundreds of readings and he even channeled information about astrology and past lives. These were things he did not believe in or know about at the time. But his readings revealed the truth of these disciplines, and he even said that our souls have spent lifetimes on different planets which he called, "planetary sojourns." Reincarnation is a belief that exists in Buddhism and Hinduism; I remember studying it when I was in college. I found it interesting that reincarnation was actually taught by St Jerome and the Catholic Church at one period of time until it was removed.

The basic premise of reincarnation is that we are a soul who continues to live on outside the body and we are reborn into a new body after death. There is a belief that karma is what brings our souls back into the physical realm. We can bring these past memories, experiences, feelings, and gifts into future lives. The people in our lives in this lifetime are those we knew before, and we can also have family karma. Sometimes we remember past lives through dreaming about different time periods in vivid detail. There are times we even have déjà vu experiences, which is a feeling that we have been somewhere or done something before. I call it a "remembrance" or "glimpse" into the past.

Our past lives and current life are intertwined, and many believe our souls choose to return back to Earth into the physical realm to learn lessons. The world is a school where our soul returns because of love and a desire to help humanity. Karma also ensures that we reap what we sow, both good and bad, whilst we are here. The law of karma is what keeps our souls coming back to repeat certain patterns. You might think to yourself that there is no way you would choose to come back to the Earth realm. I used to think this way, but now it makes sense to me after learning astrology, that there is something called destiny. I realize I chose to come here. Some events in our lives are meant to happen no matter what we do, and other things can be altered, or changed by our thoughts, words, and actions. It's a blend of a little bit of both and your astrology chart can reveal these patterns of karma that you are here to learn.

The Sixth Sense
Everyone has a sixth sense, even if you don't trust it. The key is learning how to listen within to the still, small voice which is your soul. Sixth sense is similar to intuition and can be experienced in many different ways. Your sixth sense is a spiritual gift that can manifest in the following ways:

- A gut instinct in the pit of your stomach or a strong feeling about something that stays on your mind or even repeats. You might get that feeling that you have done something before or been somewhere before. There can be a feeling that something is wrong with a family member, friend, or pet. The sixth sense can be a powerful emotion that seems to overpower you and continue to pop up in your consciousness. Don't ignore it, it's happening to get your attention or make you aware of a pattern.

- Extrasensory perception (ESP) often involves several abilities that can't be explained by science. Things like clairvoyance which can involve seeing the future through your dreams or imagination. Hearing or knowing what other people are thinking is also part of ESP and is known as telepathy.
- Sensitivity to other people's energy and the environment is another sixth sense ability. You might feel deeply connected to the thoughts and emotions of others, sensing when someone is hurting or in pain. It's important to develop self-protection and strong boundaries when dealing with people.

Your past lives and the sixth sense are connected, and many spiritual traditions confirm this. The sixth sense is thought to be an ability that every soul has, and this means that any of us can channel or connect to these memories, images, and feelings from our previous lives. Astrology can show what your past lives were and what lessons you are here to learn through the Sun sign as well as the nodes of the moon. The north node in your birth chart reveals what your soul wants to learn in this lifetime and the soul node is what your soul has already mastered. We are all here to balance the nodes of the moon and to transform our past life patterns. You can dive deeper into the importance of the nodes in our book *Astrology's Magical Nodes of the Moon*.

The Twelve Zodiac Signs

In Western astrology there are twelve signs of the zodiac. They are, in order, starting with Aries, then Taurus, Gemini, Cancer,

Leo, Virgo, Libra, Scorpio, Sagittarius, Capricorn, Aquarius, and ending with Pisces. An important thing to remember is that one of these signs will be your Sun sign, calculated by the month and day of your birth. This is the only planetary placement that shifts with our traditional calendar, making it easy to determine. This is why so many people are familiar with their Sun sign. If your birth took place on a date when the sun is in between zodiac signs or was very close to switching signs, astrologers call this being born on the cusp. If you were born on a cusp, you might resonate with traits of both signs. For instance, if you were born on April 19, then you might have personality traits of both Aries and Taurus. Typically, the sign the sun is moving into shows dominance and strength. If you're unsure of your Sun sign, your birth chart can confirm that for you. You can visit Astro.com to calculate a free birth wheel.

Each astrological sign has many components that make it unique — the sign's element, modality, ruler, and symbol bless each sign with specific gifts. We will now discuss each of the zodiac signs in detail. There will be a chart at the end of the section that sums up this information for easier reference.

Planets in Astrology

Each zodiac sign is associated with and ruled by a certain planet. There are ten main planets astrologers use in our solar system. The energy of the planet gives the zodiac sign its energy and basic personality traits. For instance, Aries is ruled by the planet Mars, which is associated with war, violence, anger, passion, sexuality, impulsiveness, impatience, and courage. Some signs share planetary rulers. Below is a list of the planets, their meanings, and what sign they are associated with.

Sign	Planet	Symbol Description	Element
Leo	Sun Rules the Sign Leo	The Sun represents your main identity, personality and ego. The Sun represents the father figure symbolically in your astrological chart. The house where the Sun is placed is where we like to shine.	Fire
Virgo Gemini	Mercury rules the Signs Virgo and Gemini	Mercury represents your thoughts, ideas, and the way you communicate. Wherever Mercury is placed is where you express yourself through writing and speaking.	Earth Air
Taurus Libra	Venus rules the Signs Taurus and Libra	Venus represents your love nature, beauty and values. Venus symbolizes the way that you express your love and feelings. Wherever Venus is placed is where you experience and seek harmony.	Earth Air
Cancer	Moon rules the Sign Cancer	The Moon represents your emotional nature and inner life. How you express your feelings depends on which house and sign the Moon is placed. The Moon represents the mother figure in your life.	Water
Aries	Mars rules the Sign Aries	Mars presents your drive, energy, aggression and impulses. Wherever Mars is placed is where you strive to succeed and are very competitive. It can also show where you experience conflict in your life.	Fire
Sagittarius	Jupiter rules the Sign Sagittarius	Jupiter represents your luck, abundance, education and travel. Jupiter shows where you benefit and experience good luck and fortune.	Fire

Capricorn	Saturn rules the Sign Capricorn	Saturn represents where you feel discipline, responsibility and where we feel restricted. Wherever Saturn is placed in your chart is where you feel uncomfortable and limited. You must strive hard to overcome this restricting energy.	Earth
Aquarius	Uranus rules the Sign Aquarius	Uranus represents your individuality, uniqueness and where you can be unusual. Anything unorthodox is Uranus energy. Uranus can represent sudden changes and the unexpected.	Air
Pisces	Neptune rules the Sign Pisces	Neptune represents your spirituality, illusions, drugs and music. Neptune shows where you find your spirituality and where you can delude yourself. It is associated with addictions such as alcohol or anything that helps you escape from reality.	Water
Scorpio	Pluto rules the Sign Scorpio	Pluto represents transformation and regeneration. Pluto is where you experience powerful spiritual and psychological changes within yourself and the environment. Pluto is an intense energy that is associated with sex, death and other people's resources.	Water

Elements in Astrology

Each zodiac sign is ruled by a certain natural element. The four elements exist in nature — fire, air, earth, and water. Fire signs are full of energy and passion; they are Aries, Leo, and Sagittarius. Air signs are Gemini, Libra, and Aquarius and they are intellectual and emotionally detached. Earth signs are practical and cautious; they are Taurus, Virgo, and Capricorn. Water signs are emotional and imaginative; Cancer, Scorpio, and Pisces are the three water signs.

Modalities and Temperament

Each sign is categorized by what astrologer's call modalities. The three distinct modalities are cardinal, fixed, or mutable. A sign's modality is significant because it reveals a deeper part of your personality that others might not see. Cardinal signs are known to be self-motivated, ambitious, activity starters, and enthusiastic about new ideas. Fixed signs are determined, strong-willed, dislike change, stable and purposeful. Mutable signs are known to be adaptable, changeable, versatile, and easygoing. When the element and modality are combined, this can tell you a lot about the zodiac sign. For example, Scorpio is fixed water. Knowing this tells you that Scorpio is an emotional, intense and strong-willed sign because fixed signs are focused on stability and water signs like to experience deep emotions and powerful connections.

Polar Opposites

Every sign has a polar opposite sign opposing it in the sky. The amazing thing is that polar opposite signs are actually very compatible. They share the same modality and a compatible element in nature. For example, Virgo and Pisces are both mutable signs and their elements of water and earth blend well together.

Modality	Key Word	Approach	Zodiac Signs
Cardinal	Initiator	Takes charge, leads, and starts new things. Need movement and challenge.	Aries, Libra, Capricorn, Cancer
Fixed	Stabilizer	Strong-willed, strong beliefs, solid, determined, calm, patient, and persistent. Doesn't like change, likes to plan and slowly move towards goals.	Taurus, Scorpio, Leo, Aquarius
Mutable	Adapter	Easygoing, flexible, adaptable, versatile, energetic, creative. Can change to adapt to situations easily and enjoys creating harmony with others.	Virgo, Pisces, Gemini, Sagittarius

***

Tarot Card Archetypes and Astrology

I remember when I purchased my first tarot deck in 1995. It was the original Rider-Waite traditional deck, and I loved it because of the specific images. I immediately saw astrological symbolism hidden within each of the cards, especially the major arcana cards. Major arcana cards are archetypes and there are twenty-two of them. Twelve of them relate to the twelve astrological signs. The other cards are associated with the ten major planets in astrology. The amazing thing I love about tarot is how the images draw out feelings from deep within. I am a visual person and images help me connect to my inner feelings. The visual imagery of the cards always makes me feel a certain way. The energy in the symbols is what connects us to the messages that we are seeking. Tarot is a tool of self-awareness just like astrology is. Depending on which images are on the cards you can intuitively know the messages without even having to refer to the book for the interpretation. I remember the first time I pulled the "Death card" and I knew that change was coming into my life.

Each astrological archetype is associated with a tarot card. Each tarot card's energy and meaning are like the zodiac sign the card is associated with. You can even see the astrology symbols on the cards. For instance, Leo is associated with the strength card that has the lion on it and Leo's symbol is the lion.

***

The graph below shows the archetype associations for easy reference.

To find out more about astrology and tarot archetypes visit www.learntarot.com and https://en.wikipedia.org/wiki/Major_Arcana.

Astrological Sign	Tarot Archetype	Key Traits
Aries	Emperor	Dynamic, Impulsive, Enthusiastic, Honest, Passionate, Blunt, Independent, Self-Centered
Taurus	Hierophant	Practical, Patient, Sensual, Reliable, Calm, Stubborn, Possessive, Persistent, Self-Indulgent
Gemini	Lovers	Communicative, Intellectual, Rational, Nervous, Versatile, Sociable, Sarcastic, Restless, Inconsistent
Cancer	Chariot	Caring, Motherly, Moody, Emotional, Protective, Imaginative, Intuitive, Possessive, Dependent, Clingy
Leo	Strength	Dramatic, Proud, Playful, Generous, Dignified, Self-Assured, Sincere, Arrogant, Domineering

Virgo	Hermit	Modest, Analytical, Perfectionist, Observant, Precise Orderly, Conscientious, Critical, Worrier, Anxious
Libra	Justice	Social, Diplomatic, Indecisive, Charming, Artistic, Romantic, Cooperative, Insincere, Harmonious
Scorpio	Death	Intense, Secretive, Compulsive, Vindictive, Healer, Subtle, Imaginative, Controlling, Jealous, Deep
Sagittarius	Temperance	Optimistic, Philosopher, Adventurous, Confident Tactless, Restless, Boastful, Traveler, Wanderer
Capricorn	Devil	Ambitious, Responsible, Rigid, Serious, Structured Hardworking, Achiever, Conventional, Pessimistic
Aquarius	Star	Impersonal, Rebellious, Humanitarian, Independent, Rational, Original, Unique, Eccentric, Detached
Pisces	Moon	Idealistic, Spiritual, Emotional, Compassionate Escapist, Receptive, Self-Sacrificing, Imaginative

Four Temperaments and Personality Theory

Historically, philosophers and seekers of knowledge tried to find answers to the basic question of "what makes people act the way they do?" Hippocrates is known as the father of medicine. He is less known for being an astrologer, but he is recognized for the famous saying, "A physician that does not have a basic knowledge of astrology, is not a physician but a fool." Ancient medicine was founded and associated with a basic knowledge of astrology. In old medical books you can see the symbols of each zodiac sign associated with the body part it rules. It is a shame that we don't always discuss these truths in our current society. But we feel that a time of change is occurring with more people seeking answers to what helps them truly heal from the past. There is more interest in the mind, body and spirit connection. Astrology is growing in popularity more than ever before. Alternative medicine and energy healing are also becoming more widespread. Many people are questioning traditional medicine and are studying astrology, energy healing, and other modalities to try to heal themselves without taking medication.

Hippocrates associated personality types into four basic areas which he called temperaments. These temperaments were used to understand personality but also used to understand the body functions and how each unique temperament healed from illness.

The four temperaments are sanguine, choleric, melancholic, and phlegmatic. Hippocrates believed we have two main temperaments that represent our personality. We can associate this theory with astrology, especially the personality traits of our Sun and Moon signs. In astrology, the sun represents our main identity, outward appearance and expression. The moon represents our deeper emotional nature, our reactions, urges, and feelings. The temperaments were energies that Hippocrates utilized and experienced with practicing medicine.

The four temperaments are very similar to the four elements in astrology. Fire is associated with the choleric temperament and signs Aries, Leo and Sagittarius. Air is related to the sanguine temperament and is associated with Gemini, Libra and Aquarius. Water is associated with the phlegmatic temperament and connected to the signs Cancer, Scorpio and Pisces. The final temperament is melancholic and is similar to the earth sign personalities of Taurus, Virgo and Capricorn.

In ancient medical astrology many believed the temperaments could become unbalanced and this affected an individual's health. These theories led to medical astrology and a belief that the four temperaments governed a person's health and disposition. Traditionally, the fire element promoted anger, the air element signified courage and optimism, the water element was related to calmness, and the earth element was related to sadness and irritability. The four temperaments and the astrological elements are connected, and this is why certain astrological signs suffer from specific personality traits that affect their mind, body and physical health.

Personality theory has identified that each person has two primary personality traits that are displayed at a higher level than the others. This is similar to the balance of astrological elements in your birth chart. Some people have a good balance of elements spread out across their chart, while others might lack an element completely. For instance, someone who lacks the water element might have difficulty expressing their feelings. If someone lacks fire in their chart then it can affect their energy and motivation. It is important to learn to balance all four elements in our lives. If you learn to balance the four elements then you will also increase your ability to balance many areas of your life. In each chapter, we will discuss the temperament associated with each astrological archetype.

Color Personality Theory

There are many personality tools that have been created to help organizations develop team building strategies. These programs are used to help supervisors understand their subordinates as well as to help co-workers to understand each other. Many work centers use the Four Lenses assessment. The assessments are used to help people understand their strengths and to help foster communication among colleagues. This team building technique can help us understand ourselves and others. You may have taken quizzes at work to find out more about your personality and work style, such as Myers-Briggs. Many people interested in astrology try to associate their astrological sign with their Myers-Briggs personality type. The Myers-Briggs theory was created with the similar knowledge of Jungian archetypes. It focuses on different things like introversion, extroversion, intuition, sensing, thinking, feeling, judging, and perceiving. For instance, an INFJ type would be introverted and need solitude. They would also be intuitive and need to trust their gut instincts. This person would make decisions based on feelings versus logic. Because they are the judging personality type, they would need structure, order, and a good routine to thrive. You can find out more about your specific personality traits online at https://www.myersbriggs.org/my-mbti-personality-type/mbti-basics/.

The personality temperament theories such as the Four Lenses focus on four main personality colors: Gold, Green, Orange and Blue. Everyone has all four colors in their personality. Although we can have stronger scores in certain personality areas, there are usually two personality colors that dominate. It's similar to the Sun sign and Moon sign traits, which are often the most dominant in our astrological chart.

Personality Color Meanings

Orange personalities are similar to the fire signs, which are Aries, Sagittarius, and Leo. They are spontaneous, need their freedom and are adventurous. Oranges thrive in crisis situations, love challenges, and resist restriction. They are known to be more extroverted and increase their energy by interacting socially with others.

Orange personality temperament traits:

Advocate Success, Appreciate Courage, Cherish Recreation, Collect Experiences, Desire Victory, Enjoy Challenges, Provide Excitement, Pursue Adventure, Respect Talent, Treasure Freedom, Trust Impulses, Want Action.

Gold personalities are very similar to the earth signs, which are Virgo, Capricorn and Taurus. They crave structure, stability, rules, order, routine, commitment, and value tradition. Golds can sometimes be micro-managers and are controlling, serious, rigid, practical, and have high standards. Gold personalities are known to be introverted and enjoy working solo on projects or assigning others tasks they don't want to do.

Gold personality temperament traits:

Advocate Discipline, Cherish Traditions, Collect Responsibilities, Desire Power, Enjoy Completion, Join Organizations, Need Order, Provide Structure, Pursue Security, Respect Achievement, Show Dedication, Treasure Appreciation, Want Rules, Trust Authority.

Blue personalities are similar to the water signs, which are Cancer, Pisces and Scorpio. They are emotional, relationship-focused, spiritual, intuitive, empathetic, imaginative, adaptable and drawn to careers where they can help people. Blue personalities are often introverted because they are empathic. Their energy gets drained easily.

Blue personality temperament traits:

Appreciate Uniqueness, Cherish Intimacy, Collect Relationships, Desire Comfort, Enjoy Communication, Join Causes, Need Harmony, Provide Intimacy, Show Kindness, Respect Integrity, Treasure Acceptance, Trust Feelings, Want Romance.

Green personalities are similar to the air signs, which are Aquarius, Libra and Gemini. They are communicators, friendly, intelligent, emotionally detached, curious, innovative, knowledgeable, system-focused and often drawn to technical occupations. Greens are known to rebel, question rules, question authority, like being right, and can think they know more than others. Green personalities are extroverted and like to socialize, network, and spend time discussing ideas with others.

Green personality temperament traits:
Advocate Solutions, Appreciate Innovation, Cherish Technology, Collect Data, Desire Efficiency, Enjoy Mysteries, Join Debates, Need Time, Provide Information, Pursue Understanding, Respect Genius, Show Composure, Treasure Autonomy, Trust Analysis, Want Competence.

Below you can find information on the four primary colors and personality traits from the Four Lenses Theory. To find out more about personality color theory visit https://fourlenses.com/.

Color	Personality Traits	Stressors
BLUE	Caring, helpful, friendly, empathetic, sensitive, relationship focused, passive, creative, imaginative, peaceful	Conflict, lying, unkindness, lack of social connections, negativity, micromanagement,
ORANGE	Brave, confident, loud, assertive, impulsive, quick, action oriented, excellent public speakers, straightforward, active, restless, energetic	Rules, being controlled, stuck at a desk, structure, rigidity, deadlines, criticism, following others, having to wait to act.
GREEN	Intelligent, focused on competence, witty, sarcastic, private, independent, inventive, innovative, sees big picture, analytical, numbers focused	Lack of independence, routine, social situations, small talk, emotions, not being in charge, relationship expectations, incompetence
GOLD	Organized, predictable, responsible, task focused, detail oriented, stable, high standards, work focused, structured, reliable	Disorganization, laziness, irresponsibility, lack of structure, unpreparedness, confusing tasks, lack of direction, change, incomplete tasks

It can be beneficial to understand the four temperaments and color personalities and their similarities to astrology. Having a basic knowledge of these different theories can help you connect many different symbols in your life and can validate your own unique personality traits and personal experiences. In each chapter, we will discuss how each color relates to each zodiac archetype and provide journal questions at the end of each chapter.

Your Top Three Archetypes

Sun Sign, Moon Sign, and Rising Sign

In this book, you will be able to find out your top three personality archetypes. In astrology, the sun, moon and rising sign are three key placements. They represent your main personality, emotional nature, physical appearance, and how you relate to the outside world. For instance, if you are a Virgo Sun, Aries Moon, and Pisces Rising your top three archetypes will be Sage, Hero, and Innocent.

Below is an easy reference guide for connecting the energy and the archetypes. To learn more about the Ryder-Waite Tarot card archetypes visit www.learntarot.com to connect with the symbolism of each tarot card and zodiac sign.

In the following chapters, we will discuss the archetypal energies and past life patterns that each zodiac sign might experience. We will give practical tips to recognize past life karmic patterns and ways to utilize your strengths.

Sun Sign	Archetype	Tarot Card	Personality Color Element Temperament	Polar Opposite Sign & Archetype	Symbol
Aries	Hero Warrior Crusader Soldier	Emperor	Orange Fire Choleric	Libra	The ram
Taurus	Realist Regular Person Solid Citizen	Hierophant	Gold Earth Melancholic	Scorpio	The bull
Gemini	Jester Comedian	Lovers	Green Air Sanguine	Sagittarius	The twins
Cancer	Caregiver Parent, Helper Supporter	Chariot	Blue Water Phlegmatic	Capricorn	The crab
Leo	Creator Artist Inventor	Strength	Orange Fire Choleric	Aquarius	The lion
Virgo	Sage Expert Planner	Hermit	Gold Earth Melancholic	Pisces	The maiden

Sun Sign	Archetype	Tarot Card	Personality Color Element Temperament	Polar Opposite Sign & Archetype	Symbol
Libra	Lover Partner Intimate	Justice	Green Air Sanguine	Aries	The scales
Scorpio	Magician Healer Visionary	Death	Blue Water Phlegmatic	Taurus	The scorpion
Sagittarius	Explorer Seeker Wanderer	Temperance	Orange Fire Choleric	Gemini	The archer
Capricorn	Ruler Boss Leader Politician	Devil	Gold Earth Melancholic	Cancer	The goat
Aquarius	Outlaw Rebel Revolutionary Misfit	Star	Green Air Sanguine	Leo	The water bearer
Pisces	Innocent Dreamer	Moon	Blue	Virgo	The fish

Chapter One

Aries the Hero

"I AM"

Keywords: Courageous, Driven, Passionate, Impulsive, Motivated, Confident

Sun Sign Dates: March 21–April 19

Temperament: Choleric

Sign Type: Fire, Cardinal

Planetary Ruler: Mars

Jungian Archetypes: Hero, Warrior, Crusader, Soldier

Tarot Card: The Emperor

Polar Opposite Archetype: Lover, Partner, Intimate

Astrology Nickname: The Warrior

Polar Opposite Sign: Libra

Symbol: The Ram

Personality Color: Orange, Extroverted

Rules: The First House; The Head and Face

Temperament: Choleric

Aries is the first sign of the zodiac. If you are an Aries, you are extroverted, confident, driven, active, rebellious, independent, and freedom-loving. Taking bold action is what you do best. You are naturally self-reliant and don't like to rely on other people. Assertiveness can sometimes make you appear bossy and dominant. You like to take charge and do what feels right in the moment. You are extroverted, friendly, and social. Your temperament seeks competition, and sports might be a way for you to release your strong physical energy.

Aries like to be in charge because you don't like to wait around. Energetic and passionate, it's hard for you to be patient. You want to act when you feel the urge to. These traits make you a natural leader and other people are drawn to your bravery. There is nothing you won't do to overcome obstacles. Driven, ambitious, and sometimes self-centered, you work hard to achieve your goals. You pursue your wants with an intense and fiery passion.

Aries are associated with the choleric temperament and are known to be energetic, strong-willed, and ambitious. Choleric people are driven, goal-oriented, and bold leaders. Achievement-focused, you enjoy competing, reaching your goals, and being successful.

You can become quite irritable and lash out at others easily. Anger is an emotion that you know well. Learning to control your anger and see it as a strength to channel into your work can energize you. Passionate in love, you enjoy a challenge and crave excitement. You enjoy the thrill of the chase and get bored easily in relationships.

Jungian Archetypes: Hero, Soldier and Warrior

Aries is associated with the hero archetype; no wonder you like to lead. Your confidence and bravery help you overcome many obstacles. When others run away from crisis or danger, you charge straight into it. You seek excitement and adventure in life. You need to feel alive and experience passion. Like a knight riding on a white horse, you want to save the helpless and rescue others from danger. Taking risks is where you function best and when you can experience heightened intensity. You thrive in crisis situations and have a natural gut instinct that helps you know what to do instinctively. Many Aries individuals are drawn to law enforcement, military careers, firefighting and emergency medical careers. You might enjoy owning your own business and working in sales, marketing, coaching, and finance.

Aries are natural leaders and seek out positions of power. You make excellent heroes because you don't do it for the glory, you actually do care about people. Born with natural communication skills you are able to champion others to follow you into battle. People look up to you because of your confidence. Blunt, straightforward and honest people never have to guess where you stand with them.

Passionate, you like to be in love and express passionate feelings. You are quite changeable in relationships though — one minute you can be in love with your soul mate and the next day you might want to be free. Being self-reliant and being independent are the most important things to you. Sometimes you will cut ties if you feel tied down or controlled. You like the chase and grow disinterested if things are too easy or comfortable in love. Strong and independent people impress you and they might keep your heart forever.

Tarot Card Archetype: The Emperor

The Emperor card in the tarot deck is associated with the Aries archetype. In the traditional Ryder-Waite image you can see the symbol of the ram on the throne. Aries sits confidently holding on to the sword, ready to decide on something or maybe even go into battle. The Emperor symbolism portrays a bold, brave, courageous, and direct persona. Just like Aries traits, the Emperor is not afraid of making decisions and fighting for what is right. You are a charismatic leader, mentor, and motivator. There is no one who will fight harder to achieve what they want than an Aries. Natural leaders, Arians are put in positions of authority because of their ability to speak the brutal truth. Honest to a fault, sometimes your words can cut like a knife. Impulsiveness can sometimes lead to foolhardy actions. You can move on too fast and leave a lot of rubble behind you. But people will always know how you really feel. Aries, like the Emperor energy, sees through facades. There is an intense dislike for superficiality and fakeness. You often root for the underdog because of your respect for people who work hard for what they have.

Sign Type: Fire Element

Aries is a fire sign and creates an enthusiastic, optimistic, and confident personality. The fire element ignites a great passion and desire to achieve your goals. You are driven to succeed and to get what you want. Fear is not something that stops you! There is a fierceness and competitiveness that pushes you forward. Once you make up your mind you drive full force into battle and no one can stop you. If someone gets in your way, you will bypass them and fight even harder. You are very in-tune with your own needs and often focus on yourself. It's difficult for you to rely on others because you would rather do things yourself. Being self-reliant and independent helps you feel a sense of control. Happiness often comes through achievement and pushing yourself to face challenges. You like to compete and winning brings you even more energy to keep going. The fire element makes you resilient and blesses you with an ability to overcome difficult life situations quickly.

Personality Color: Orange

Aries energy represents everything that orange personalities respect. You have the ability to think on your feet. Physical touch, intimacy, and self-expression are important. Boldness, positivity, brashness, action, and confidence. A childlike innocence and a need for adventure make Aries fun to be around. Orange personalities thrive when they experience change, crisis, and challenges. You excel at sports and doing anything that gets your heart racing makes you feel alive. Competitive at heart, hobbies such as bungee jumping, skydiving, skiing, and rock-climbing interests you. Being a part of a team can also bring happiness. Solo activities can also be fulfilling such as hunting, fishing, or hiking in nature.

You like to be spontaneous and are not the type to plan ahead. Living in the moment is what you do best. Following your inner instincts often leads to success. Natural public speakers, Aries are born with a charming ability to sell anything. Orange personalities share similar personality traits with the Aries archetype. You value autonomy, freedom, and having freedom of movement. Being able to be self-reliant and make your own choices brings happiness and contentment. Your temper can flare and you will stand up for yourself. You might lash out in anger, but you get over it quickly. Your ability to move on fast and focus on the future is a true gift.

The Aries Current Life Span

If you were born under the sign of Aries, you need a vast territory from which to manifest your mental energy and intuition. You possess a restless spirit that enjoys being challenged. Your competitive nature offers you an endless amount of energy to reach your goals. You appreciate your talents being recognized. The traditional astrology mantra for your sign is "I am." Your identity is important to you in that a strong sense of self propels you into action. People able to notice your abilities draw you closer.

You likely enjoy people with lively personalities. You prefer individuals to get to the point quickly in communicating their expectations of you. Entering relationships quickly is a trait of your sign. Sometimes you can leave a trail of lovers behind who had no idea why you left so quickly. With experience you learn to become less impulsive in rushing into a relationship. Learning more about commitment and dedicating yourself to one person can help you achieve more than you think. It's okay to allow yourself to rely on other people and remember that you don't always have to do everything by yourself.

You might be more sensitive than people realize until they get to know you. Your emotional nature can be covered with an external persona of strength so much of the time that outside observers don't detect a strong feeling in you. Deep down you are loving, affectionate, and passionate.

Learning patience with others brings them closer. You prefer people who respect your need for freedom. A lover or friend able to understand your spontaneous ideas excites you. You need people who allow you autonomy and those who don't try to control you. You respect people who work as hard as you do and those who are willing to take risks.

Your identity is a special connection to your spirit and your intuitive perceptions. In many ways it is a sacred part of you whether you reveal this openly to others or keep it hidden until you trust someone. People who empower you become close allies. You have a special way of elevating your self-confidence. Aries people, through their own intuition and mental insights, discover the key to the portal that opens to the heart and the fountain of your love.

When you pace yourself and learn to reflect in a meditative way, your intuitive awareness makes itself known to you. This energy is a deeper part of your identity that is readily available to you. When you discover this empowering resource, there is no past life pattern discussed in this book that can maintain a hold on your mental and emotional worlds.

The Aries Past Life Karmic Patterns

Each of us has brought past life memory patterns into this lifetime with us. You likely will not find each of the following karmic patterns being discussed as a regular part of your own experience. Pay special attention to the ones that seem like a piece of your current journey. Nothing written by the authors in this book is meant to pass judgment on you. Think of this as a path to personal empowerment. In acknowledging a past life pattern, you are taking the first step to transform energy into an enlightening insight. Tapping into your natural intuition and gut instincts make it easier for you to let go of the past.

As an Aries, in following the guidance of your sixth sense, your boldness will inspire you to rise above karmic patterns that could be keeping you from fulfilling relationships and inner harmony. It can take much practice to overcome a karmic pattern. Don't get discouraged if you fall back into a behavior after you acknowledge its presence in your life. This is a typical occurrence for everyone. It is a learning experience. The important thing is to keep trying to improve and grow.

Sixth Sense Intuitive Perceptions:
Paths to Transforming Karmic Patterns

It takes more energy to cling to a karmic pattern than to let it go. The relief when one of these past, shadowy patterns is conquered is well worth the effort. The good news is that as an Aries you are born resilient and with an uncanny ability to push forward quickly. This enables you to focus on the future more than other signs and to release the past. In some ways you could feel like a relationship has had a rebirth. Your mind might experience a recharge. You likely will wonder why it took so long to dispense with the negative hold on you that was interfering with forming good harmony in your important relationships.

Lack of Assertion

There might have been incarnations where you said yes too many times when you really wanted to say no. If this sounds familiar as a regular impulse in this life when interacting with others, then this is very possibly a repeating theme that followed you into this incarnation. It can easily throw your relationships out of balance. You might try to over-assert yourself and maintain freedom at all costs. Healthy relationships involve understanding other people's needs. You might focus fully on your own needs, and this can make others perceive you as selfish. Establishing equality you desire with others is lacking in this behavior. Your personal happiness is not where you want it to be if you are giving to the extreme or always doing what you want. The give and take in your partnerships might need an adjustment. Balance is the key to listening to your inner voice.

This karmic pattern often attracts people to you that have controlling behaviors. Your own goals are not seen as important to a person extremely focused on their own dreams. It can feel like a real slap in the face if your own hopes and wishes are not valued. Aries thrive on having their ideas encouraged by others. Your fiery spirit evaporates into steam if you become too trapped by this past-life theme.

Your sixth sense intuition can guide you to overcome the Lack of Assertion by practicing putting yourself at the front of the line. You need to place a higher value on your own needs. It will take some regular practice to accomplish this. Eventually you will feel more empowered to the level you need to reach. If it feels awkward at first to be more assertive, don't worry. It is a common experience to take two steps forward and one step back with this past life pattern. If you are often in the company of people with strong personalities, it could take a few tries to speak up more forcefully to have your voice heard. As an Aries, you came into this life to definitely have an equal seat at the table. There might be a person you need to drop as a friend or at least make it known that their way of treating you is no longer acceptable. Sometimes getting away from the line of fire when people are not looking out for your best interests is one of the paths to seeing your way out of this pattern. It might sound strange but learning to be more self-focused and in tune with your own needs will help you achieve your goals.

Playing the Blame Game

Having faith in your sixth sense intuition can reverse the impact of the Playing the Blame Game energy pattern. This is a past life pattern that can make you constantly blame people for your problems which takes away from your road to personal empowerment. Rather than getting caught up in regularly finding fault with others, you'll benefit more from paying attention to solutions to problems. This is not saying you should feel overly responsible for situations not going well. Your Aries mental strength is energized in a more productive way when you don't allow yourself to become ensnared by the entanglement of this karmic net. Your own goals get diluted if you put excess energy into holding others too accountable for what they seem to be doing to interfere with your plans. Believing more in your own ability to fulfill your goals is far better than looking to accuse others of blocking your road to success.

Trusting your sixth sense intuition can lift you above the negative pull in the Playing the Blame Game. There are times accepting responsibility for your own actions keeps this pattern away from you. It often takes two people to contribute to a problem but then again it requires the cooperation of both individuals to right the course. You will find your relationships with others have less tension when you are willing to work toward more productive results. Casting blame is usually a defense mechanism you use to deal with conflict in relationships. If you want to receive more support for your own goals, a good way to do this is to let go of a tendency to accuse others of being the source of the difficulties in your life. You will experience much more fulfillment in your relationships when you make a serious commitment to releasing this karmic pattern.

Power Struggles
In this pattern left over from past incarnations, it can sometimes be experienced in the way you relate to others like a tug of war. Your ideas can forcefully clash with people. Bluntness and cutting words can set other people off. There is a way to be kind and direct, it just takes a little bit of practice. Your negotiating

tactics may be missing. There could have been past incarnations where you did not believe in compromise. The "might makes right" was your mantra. If this pattern of behavior gets awakened in this lifetime it tends to alienate those you want to remain close to. Creating win-win solutions remains out of reach if you lock horns endlessly with others. Much time gets wasted and you can end up very frustrated. Sometimes winning becomes too important to you and does not help you establish the victory formula for relationship success. You might wonder why you have a trail of upset friends and lovers who no longer want to interact with you. The harmony you seek will remain beyond your reach when allowing this past life shadow to cover your clearer mental and intuitive perceptions.

When you embrace the inner clarity found in your sixth sense intuition, the Power Struggles lesson and relationships improve. Conquering this past life pattern comes down to knowing how to use that powerful Aries inner strength. The key here is to not make people feel undervalued or dismissed. It will take some practice in realizing when to push hard for your own ideas and when to pause and carefully consider options being presented to you. Getting your own way at all costs will put others on the defensive. Learning to listen and slow down your mind puts you on the road to great relationship harmony. If you pay more attention to others in the moment and read their body language, you can adapt to the needs of the situation. People are more apt to admire you if you meet them halfway when you pitch them a plan. You will find it easier to attract love, intimacy, and emotional support through showing humility alongside a show of power. Remember, you are not being weak in considering other people's points of view.

Intense Adrenaline Rush

Your sign is known for moving fast. In past incarnations there could have been a tendency to move quickly into romantic relationships or other types of situations. If you have gotten into trouble by throwing caution to the wind this might be an instinct still influencing your actions. Your assertiveness and fast-paced energy can take you to new creative heights. There are times this same energy does not serve you as well in relationships. You could be too trusting of others at the beginning of relationships to the point of lacking clear judgment. If you feel chemistry and passion for someone, you often dive headfirst without thinking. Your desire to feel passion and romance can overtake your sense of reality. You might get caught up in strong emotions and want to act on them.

As an Aries, the universe does bless you with incredible energy. It is the excitement of meeting someone new that can fog your perceptions if you get in too much of a hurry. Another side of this pattern is changing directions so quickly that it confuses others. You might show a lack of consistency to the point that people will not know what to expect from you. This behavior can make others feel like they can't rely or depend on you to be there when they need it.

Your sixth sense intuition can tell you when to slow down enough to calm the intensity found in the Intense Adrenaline Rush karmic pattern. If this pattern is still in your memory bank from past lives and has become activated in your current life, it can be brought under control. How might you accomplish this? Slowing down before always relying on snap decisions is the first step.

Taking your time to process choices, whether it involves a relationship, career move, or another big decision goes far to heal this pattern. Taking extra time to get to know someone before leaping too fast into a relationship can open your eyes more clearly as to whether you want to make a commitment or not. Also, it is vital in maintaining a successful relationship to include a partner or significant other in important decisions. Aries loves spontaneity. But constantly making snap decisions can disrupt the harmony in a relationship. If you keep others in the loop about your plans you will find people more supportive of your goals.

Hiding From the Truth

It could be that in some past incarnations you did not accept criticism very well. This was especially true when someone pointed out how certain behaviors were repeated no matter how many times you were told they were upsetting. If this karmic pattern is awakened in this lifetime, it can add a great amount of tension to your relationships with lovers, friends, family members, or work colleagues. If you have been repeating actions that irritate those closest to you without making any adjustments, you will alienate people. Denial only serves to enlarge problems. Refusing to listen or engage in clear communication creates distance with others. Your sense of fulfillment will eventually feel much lower than you desire if you continue to react aggressively to other people's feedback.

There is another way this past life pattern may have manifested. It is very possible in past lifetimes that you have been a victim too many times of the bad actions of others who had no regard for your own needs. In other words, you did not make it known how you really felt when mistreated by others. You might have stifled your anger and refused to speak up at that moment. Often the underlying deeper emotion found is hurt, and anger is just a reaction to the hurt feelings.

If you listen to that inner voice of sixth sense intuition you are less likely to engage in the Hiding From the Truth karmic pattern. This karmic theme has its roots in denial. Nobody is that happy about having their actions criticized. But acting like there is not a problem when there is one, usually makes the problem bigger. It can also cause further resentment and frustration. However, sometimes it only takes you displaying that you are attempting to change a behavior to show you are listening. This is a good first step to alleviating stress in a relationship. It is amazing how honest communication makes this past life pattern evaporate as though it never existed. You will notice people will respond positively when you show a commitment to surrender behaviors that only serve to alienate others. When you stop trying to hide from the truth, a feeling of liberation takes its place.

Frozen Momentum

If this pattern follows you into this incarnation, you can stop pursuing new endeavors too quickly. This is giving up on a plan soon after you take a step towards it. You are backing off likely due to a loss of self-confidence. It could even be leaving a new relationship before it has a chance to deepen. There are different reasons this might occur if the pattern gets awakened regularly. One is a fear of failure. In a relationship it could happen when someone wants to learn more about your emotional nature. Your reaction could be to leave. You could be with someone that would be good for you but your reluctance to invest enough time can be a problem. You might also not want to feel tied down or have someone become too dependent on you. Another reason for an early exit from a relationship or a goal is an inner restlessness. Giving situations enough time to turn into a solid commitment does not appeal to you. The idea that you might be missing out on meeting someone new or experimenting with a new idea is more exciting. This may constantly keep you from settling into a long-term relationship or stable work opportunity.

If lessons are learned it can help with the Frozen Momentum Pattern and it will be a way to prevent this pattern from emerging. You will then enjoy a greater chance to rub against the warm feet of a potentially fulfilling partner. Time together with a lover is essential to know the real depth of a relationship. If you stay longer in a relationship and truly explore a potential deeper love with someone it could turn out to be a pleasant surprise. A relationship needs time to reveal its deeper rewards. The longer you trust the commitment and the bond between you and another person, the more it grows in trust and strength. This is a past life karmic pattern that will lessen its hold on your mind when you learn to appreciate the loving support that closeness with a person can deliver. It comes down to valuing intimacy more than giving into running away. Overcoming feelings of being vulnerable will also help you overcome this pattern. The roots of a relationship grow quickly when you stick around to enjoy the progressive growth of being with someone. All of your creative energy gets inspired when rejuvenated with your sixth sense inner knowing. That reluctance to launch a dream will seem like a distant memory!

Extreme "Me Focus"

This karmic pattern is colored with too much I am-ness. If you are in the habit of making use of this behavior, you will certainly lose sight of the needs of others. This can cause great tension with people from all walks of life. It can influence your family, friends, romantic partnerships, and work relationships. A loss of awareness in what people close to you need weakens your bond with them. The support you want for your own goals will be much less than you desire. If others feel you are selfish or lack empathy, they will withdraw from you. Aries energy offers you an intense drive to pursue your own dreams. This self-driven enthusiasm can become so extreme that you can easily lose sight of what others might need from you. This pattern of behavior can cause a loved one to feel like you are not listening to their need for you to pay attention to them. Other people might feel that you don't truly care about their needs. You might even be labeled as unreliable, self-centered, and immature.

By using your sixth sense, the Extreme "Me Focus" past life pattern can be overcome by facing the fact you are not paying equal attention to the important individuals in your life. It takes some time to turn a large ship around and likewise it will need some effort to conquer this karmic pattern. Communication is one of the most important things in a relationship. If you accept the need to become a better listener, you will soon realize you are at least halfway beyond the grip of this pattern. Aries is a self-driven sign. The same strength you acquired at birth from this bold fire sign only needs to be focused on being more attentive to others. It just takes a small shift in your awareness and a little bit of effort. This does not require you to sacrifice your own goals. If you put in the determination to align your vision of today and tomorrow with that of another person, each of you benefits from a mutually healthy and mature interaction.

Space Invasion

If you don't give people enough room to be themselves then it might be due to the resurfacing of a karmic pattern. It will make others uncomfortable if you are constantly invading someone's desire to make their own decisions. You can feel impatient waiting for others to take action, so you decide for them. Often you can overwhelm others with your intensity and bossy approach. You mean well and are often just trying to help others make a decision. In fact, in-action can frustrate you greatly. It makes compromise easier to attain when valuing the independence of others. Trust issues are sometimes what launches this past life tendency, and it resurfaces into the current incarnation. The more you move onto the turf boundaries of someone in an unsolicited way, the more likely you will be met with anger or some form of resistance. An inner insecurity could be at the root of this pattern launching itself into this life. This pattern or karmic shadow will create great distance between you and others.

It is also possible it is your territory that is being invaded. There are times when you are not using that Aries assertion that this pattern occurs. You could be attracting individuals with very little awareness that your independence must be respected. These situations are teaching you how to speak up and use your voice.

When you tap into that river of sixth sense intuition within you, the Space Invasion past life pattern can be alleviated. You can then make sure you give others plenty of breathing room to feel free to exert their own version of independence. Sometimes this behavior is caused by feelings of inner insecurity. This can cause you not to trust people. Relying on yourself is what is most comfortable but there are times you will need others. You will find intimacy easier to establish when you don't just show someone that you trust them, but you prove to them that you appreciate their support. Relinquishing a need to control someone sets a relationship free to bring you much more fulfillment. The happiness you seek resides in giving a partner plenty of room to explore their own goals. It is then you will receive plenty of invitations to join those you love in their space.

People are more likely to reveal their inner world to you when you let them take the initiative to share their life with you rather than feeling like they are being too pushed to do so. It is tempting as an Aries to push for more territory. That is a natural instinct with your sign. Just beware of the boundary lines and your relationships will flow more smoothly.

If you were the person in past incarnations that had their space over-invaded, using your sixth sense instincts can make this pattern magically disappear. You now define your boundaries clearly. Your own goals will not get lost in the wind and swallowed by the demands of other people. In past incarnations you may have attracted strong-willed individuals who had a way of superimposing their own hopes and dreams over your own. In the current incarnation your self-determination to keep this pattern away does rely on your mental strength and your sixth sense awareness. If this past-life influence rings a bell with you, then it is important to remain vigilant and not let this energy from the past into your current life. You will then enjoy balance and harmony in your relationships as well as feeling whole again.

Extreme Competitiveness

Being competitive comes with being an Aries. Having the fiery and highly energetic Mars as your ruling planet goes far in explaining your attraction to competition. If you must always win an argument in your social interactions, it could be due to a past life pattern making an entrance into this life. The end result could be you push people away. Winning at all costs can cause you to lose valuable people in your life. You can end up feeling very lonely. Give and take as a philosophy is a wiser idea to promote relationship peace and harmony. There is nothing wrong with being a competitive person. It is that drive that can bring career success and push your momentum toward a goal with great enthusiasm. In your personal interactions it can even give you the self-confidence to meet new friends, business associates and lovers. If this past life pattern has resurfaced in the current life, you need to express a less feisty way of having to come out the winner. Toning down the constant need to be a winner promotes relationship harmony. Remember the saying, "it doesn't matter if you win or lose, it's how you play the game." You can enjoy competition much more when it's shared with others in healthy ways.

In projecting and trusting your sixth sense, the Extreme Competitiveness past life karmic pattern can be resolved through becoming more sensitive to how your actions impact others. This is a type of energy that, when directed in a positive way toward your goals, is a wonderful ally. It only takes redirecting this part of your natural competitive expression with greater awareness. There will be occasions when you are so forcefully convinced your ideas are the best that by taking a pause, even if for a matter of minutes, it can put others at ease. If you stay patient and think before acting on impulse you will win great appreciation from those people you want to bring closer in your life. Your Aries strength can arouse a competitive spirit from people. Competition can empower you. Overpowering someone constantly to meet your needs can be transformed into a win-win philosophy.

Sabotaging a Relationship

If you regularly try to find ways to end a relationship, even if there are no problems, this could be due to a past life karmic pattern. Sometimes this is caused by a fear of the relationship failing at some point in the future. It could be you don't have the self-confidence that you are deserving of a long-term successful relationship. Or it could be a feeling that you are missing out on a better partner by remaining in the current situation. You might be looking for a perfect partner, which does make for a problem. Or you may be demanding perfection from yourself that is impossible to deliver. You might also grow bored if you feel there is not a magnetic attraction or chemistry. It's important to remember that it's natural and normal for strong feelings to level out. Excitement in a relationship is good at the beginning but after a time it is healthy for emotions to balance out. If you are purposely looking to sabotage a relationship, you will never really learn if you are with the right person. If you focus on negative outlooks for a relationship, the end result is not going to be fulfilling.

In introducing your sixth sense into this behavior, the Sabotaging a Relationship pattern can be overcome by being willing to take the risk to stay longer in a relationship that has promise of a solid future. You might be surprised that actually establishing a commitment with someone is the path to healing this past life pattern. Or you and a partner might decide that in the end the relationship needs to be ended or perhaps it may remain a friendship. The important thing is that you are releasing a pattern by going in a new direction. It will become a learning experience and convince you that a deeper commitment will give you the insight not to leave a good relationship before you give it a fair chance. If this pattern is recurring in this lifetime, it might be due to a feeling of divine discontent, meaning you are in search of a perfect person. It could take some reality testing to find your way to accept there is no perfect person. A fear of a relationship failing as it begins can be brought under control by developing a positive attitude. Your belief in your ability to work together with a lover gains strength if you choose to stay long enough in a relationship to let it reveal itself.

Misguided Anger

Anger is a powerful emotion. There are times when anger is an appropriate response. If you find yourself exploding suddenly at friends, family or loved ones on a regular basis it is possible this is a past life pattern that has planted itself in your memory bank. If you are holding on to anger for extended time periods it can rush out unexpectedly when you least anticipate it. It could be a holdover from past incarnations needing to be overcome. If you feel that anger will help you get your own way in relationships it can form a feeling of resentment from those people you need in your life. If you don't channel your anger productively, this can be an energy working against you. Anger is usually a result of feeling hurt by something or even frustrated that something is not happening fast enough. You need to remember that other people might not be comfortable with things happening in the moment, they need more time to think through things before making decisions.

When you trust your sixth sense the Misguided Anger past life pattern has a much better chance for you to express a clearer channeling of your powerful emotions. When anger is used as a weapon to force your opinions on others, it has a disruptive effect on relationships. Trusting that you can openly negotiate with someone for what you need is a better path to choose. Compromise is often the ticket to getting your own goals supported. Returning the favor in helping someone else achieve their own goals gets you the same help in return. When making use of your intuitive sixth sense you find greater awareness in not wrongly using anger to intimidate others. You can understand that anger is better turned into working passionately to achieve mutual understanding in your social interactions.

Your sixth sense can help you in another way. It is possible this pattern shows its face as you're hiding your anger over a situation that can potentially explode onto the scene of an unrelated circumstance. That held back anger is sure to make itself known in ways you might not be able to control. It is better to let your views be known, even if they don't always seem well received by others. It lessens the intensity of your emotions when you are more open with people. This allows for a more balanced way of expressing how you feel.

Promises Not Delivered

Fire signs like yourself tend to exaggerate your capabilities at times. It is possible, as a past life tendency in some incarnations, that you promised more than you could accomplish. This in itself is not a bad thing because it is that extra thrust of self-confidence that catapults you to do great things. But you can frustrate and anger people if you don't follow through on a regular basis with promises. There may be specific behaviors you have pledged to change but fail over and over to do so. It might be true as a karmic pattern that you tend to attract individuals into your current life who are not completing what they intend to do for you. You can feel as though you are not valued when people exhibit this behavior.

When tuning into your sixth sense, the Promises Not Delivered past life pattern is less of a pull on you if you are more reasonable about your capabilities. Sometimes the restlessness inherent in a fire sign like Aries will distract you from finishing a plan. If you anticipate a delay in what you have pledged to accomplish for someone it helps to let them know in advance to avoid disappointing them. Communication is valuable in keeping others on the same page with you. The more you live up to your promises, people will do the same for you.

Your sixth sense can help you master another possible feature of this pattern which is attracting people who don't follow through on promises. In other words, in past incarnations you frequently allowed this to happen to you. Making sure you assertively call people out on this behavior goes far in resolving this pattern. Tap into your natural bluntness and use your direct approach to address these issues as they arise. Clear and practical communication can help you overcome this pattern.

If you identify with any of the karmic patterns discussed try not to worry. There is a portal to walk through that can help you find your way out of a pattern. Sometimes a karmic past life pattern can feel like your mind is lost in a maze. You can be searching for the exit out of the pattern and can feel lost. It is possible your conscious mind is not aware you are regularly engaging in a karmic pattern in the way you relate to others. Hopefully this book will bring greater confidence in facing a pattern so you can explore how to escape from its grasp. Awakening to the reality of a karmic pattern is the first step along a new path to a more productive use of this energy.

The Aries Reward for Using Your Sixth Sense Intuitive Perception to Solve Karmic Patterns

"I Won't Back Down" is a song by the American rock star, Tom Petty. This song encompasses your resilient energy. Facing the challenge presented by a karmic pattern is something you can overcome and master. Each step forward might be accompanied by two steps back in resolving a past life pattern. Be patient and continue to work hard in defeating it. If you persist on your quest to overcome a karmic pattern it will summon the Aries warrior courage to emerge. It does take some fortitude to face a karmic pattern. The bravery you possess will help you fight to win this battle. Each successful step along your life journey toward a new understanding of a past life pattern can be empowering.

If you identified with any of the Aries karmic patterns discussed, try not to worry. The important thing is to become more aware of any pattern that has followed you into this lifetime. Recognizing your personality traits and behaviors will help you address them. It does take some effort and determination to change a pattern into a more positive part of your self-expression. As an Aries, you have the drive, determination, and passion to overcome negative patterns. Tapping into patience and easing restlessness can help. Taking the time to retrain your mind in obtaining a more productive expression of a past life pattern pays dividends. You will find greater fulfillment in all of your relationships.

Aries The Hero Journal Prompts

1. How do you feel when you see the Aries image?
2. What Aries traits do you resonate with?
3. How can you be more patient with yourself and others?
4. How do you handle your anger?
5. What are some ways you can be less impulsive and more patient?
6. What are some positive goals you want to accomplish?
7. What past life patterns have you experienced?

Chapter Two

Taurus the Real Person

"I HAVE"
Keywords: Strong-Willed, Patient, Calm, Stable, Determined, Practical, Stamina
Sun Sign Dates: April 20–May 20
Temperament: Melancholic
Sign Type: Earth, Fixed
Planetary Ruler: Venus
Jungian Archetype: The Real Person, Solid Citizen
Tarot Card: The Hierophant
Polar Opposite Archetype: The Explorer
Astrology Nickname: The Builder
Polar Opposite Sign: Scorpio
Symbol: The Bull
Personality Color: Gold, Introverted
Rules: The Second House; Neck, Shoulders

Temperament: Melancholic

Taurus is the second sign of the zodiac. You are introverted, value beauty, a bit shy, slow to change, and emotionally connected to the past. Once you make up your mind about something it's almost impossible to change it. Determined to succeed, you like the security that money and material possessions can bring. Not only does having money bring a sense of comfort, but you can also enjoy the power that money can provide. Attachment to material things and a nostalgic personality can make it hard for you to release the past. It's not uncommon for you to work hard, plotting, and planning your goals.

Taking things slow and resisting change helps you feel in control. It's not easy for you to take advice from others and it's because you think you know best. It's important to remember that there are times that other people's ideas can help you. Listening to and valuing other people's opinions will improve your relationships. With people you care about you are sensual, affectionate, loyal, and committed. Your temperament seeks harmony, comfort, and safety.

Taurus likes to be prepared, and you can find it challenging when things don't go as planned. Competitive and strategic, patience is your virtue. Being slow to do things and taking baby steps can make others think you are lazy or uninterested. You just want to wait before acting. Your earthy, grounded nature helps you make practical decisions. Feeling out of control or rushed can make you feel uneasy. Driven, ambitious, and sometimes self-centered, you work hard to achieve your goals. You pursue achievement and success with deliberate action.

Taurus is associated with the melancholic temperament and is known to be reflective, thoughtful, and timid. Melancholic people are sensitive and easily connect with the thoughts and feelings of others. You value stability in love and relationships. Commitment, dedication, and patience come naturally to you. Possessive at times, you can be jealous but are a devoted partner. Spending time with your loved ones is paramount. Although it's also important that you have solitude because it enables you to process your thoughts and feelings. Melancholic personality types have high standards. You can be a worrier and dwell on things that didn't go right and feel anxiety about change. Change can be hard, and you often resist it. Born with high standards, you need to learn to be less critical of yourself and others. Being more open-minded to other people's opinions will help improve all areas of your life.

Melancholic people are peaceful, calm, and benefit through experiencing the senses. You can enjoy spending time in nature with trees and water. Your sense of smell, taste, sound, and touch is extraordinary. It's not uncommon if you have unique sensitivities to certain foods, smells, and environments. Maybe even some underlying allergies. Getting fresh air, walking in the woods, and spending time gardening can be soothing and healing. Doing activities that help ground you will benefit your health.

Jungian Archetype: Regular Person, Realist, Solid Citizen

Taurus is associated with the regular person archetype. You have a down-to-earth and grounded energy. Reliable, practical, and approachable you attract people easily. You have a friendly, kind, and calming personality. Trustworthy and loyal, there is nothing you won't do for those you care about. Dependable, hardworking, and competitive, you enjoy stability. People look to you for honest and realistic feedback. Your practical side is able to compartmentalize work, business, and personal issues. You are solid, stable, and at times fiercely stubborn. Being strong-willed can benefit you in some ways but it can cause conflict in relationships. You are traditional and have strong values.

Taureans are excellent problem solvers — you can see a practical solution to most problems. Simple, normal and balanced, you don't allow your emotions to take over. This archetype enhances Taureans' ability to be genuine and honest with others. As a regular person you can relate to the practical needs of others and enjoy everyday pleasures.

Disorganization can disrupt your equilibrium and cause extreme anxiety. You are able to help support people who are upset, emotional, and overwhelmed. There is an inherent ability you possess to socialize with people from all walks of life. As a regular person, Taurus has common sense and believes in being patient. You are goal-focused and enjoy making money because money brings safety and security. Having your basic needs met is crucial for lasting happiness. You don't want to struggle to survive or pay your bills. Saving for a rainy day will help you find a sense of peace.

Rules, routine, and a structured work environment are where you thrive best. As a diligent worker you often take on a lot of responsibilities and prioritize tasks seamlessly. It might take you more time to accomplish certain tasks, but that is because of your thorough and detailed work style. Taureans are also very talented and can have artistic gifts such as singing or enjoy playing an instrument.

Tarot Card Archetype: Hierophant

The Hierophant card in the tarot deck is associated with the Taurus archetype. This image symbolizes authority, tradition, and respect. Just like the sign Taurus, there is a strong belief system and structured way of doing things. Taurus sits on the throne with a sense of purpose, fairness, and strong traditional beliefs. The Hierophant symbolizes order, spiritual guidance, and structure. Born with strong religious beliefs and values, you are often devoted or believe in practicing a traditional religion. You are a natural teacher, enjoy learning, and often seek out the reasons why people believe what they do. Pursuing knowledge, gathering information, maintaining morals, rules, and developing a sense of loyalty radiate from this card. Just like you, the Hierophant wants to feel grounded and know what is going to happen next. Doing what is conventional and what makes sense logically can help you find stability. Taureans, like the Hierophant, can be judgmental, strong-willed, resistant to change, disciplined, and conservative in their views.

Sign Type: Earth Element

Taurus is an earth sign which makes you practical, reliable, and dependable. Once you decide to do something, you work diligently to achieve your goals. You are calm, sensitive, and need structure in your life. Accomplishing tasks and being organized are critical for your self-worth. You value things that are lasting, secure, and reliable. Happiness often comes through achievement and pushing yourself to study, learn, and use your skills in the real world. You like to make money not only because you like things, but because it brings comfort. You can achieve financial stability easily because of your dedication and planning. You work slowly, thinking about all things that might happen and plotting the most realistic outcome. Resistance to change makes it difficult for when things don't go as planned. Taking risks does not come easily and you prefer to keep things exactly how they are. You don't like to act on impulse and often make decisions on practicality above emotion. Maintaining comfort is more important to you than excitement or strong emotions. If you feel unsettled or rushed there can be resistance. There are times you might feel anxious or stressed, especially if you are in an unstable, toxic, or intensely emotional environment.

Personality Color: Gold

Taurus is the spokesperson for the personality color gold. Earthy, stable, and calm there is not a lot that disturbs your peace. You value tradition, rules, and keeping things in order. To feel secure, you often can be found trying to control your environment and finances. You like structure, reliability, and predictability. As a gold personality, having a routine helps you focus on getting tasks accomplished. Disorganization can cause chaos and make you feel unsettled. You might have a desire to control situations and establish a sense of authority over others. Golds make excellent administrators and enjoy enforcing the rules. Being in charge is where you shine.

Anything that is sloppy, disorganized, or rushed disturbs your equilibrium. It is important that you stay firmly grounded. Being disciplined, loyal and responsible are your core strengths.

Focusing on practical duties, making checklists, and being productive helps you achieve your goals. You like to aim to reach all your goals slowly. Patient, calm, and committed, other people can depend on you to keep your word. When you say you are going to do something then you do it.

The only problem is that you can get so set in your ways that you refuse to listen to other people's views. Sometimes it's difficult for you to accept new ideas or make needed changes. You need to remember that others do things differently and the traditional ways of doing things are not always as effective. Be more open-minded and accepting of other people's point of view. Your relationships will improve when you try to understand others' motives. People who work too quickly can make you feel uneasy and uncomfortable. It's just not your style to rush, but these individuals can actually help open up new ideas and ways of having more fun. If you are able to let go of stubbornness and do things differently, then you will find that your relationships with co-workers, friends, and family will improve.

The Taurus Current Life Span

If you were born under the sign of Taurus, you like people who don't rush you into a relationship. If you are already in a committed partnership, you appreciate someone supporting your goals. In traditional astrology, the keyword phrase for your sign is, "I have." People who are generous with their resources warm your mind and heart. You feel closer to individuals who value your ideas and insights. Being able to celebrate milestones in your life with a special person is a deep desire. You need affection and touch in a relationship. Holding hands, hugs, and physical intimacy are crucial to your happiness.

You value loyalty and friendship but grow impatient with those who take too much from you and give little in return. If your trust is betrayed it is difficult to continue to want the person in your life. Because you are connected to the past it can be difficult for you to forgive and let things go. You can display a wonderful way of going the extra mile to help a close friend in need of your help. Making others feel supported and safe is your superpower.

Your values must be respected by others. People don't have to adopt your belief system but gain your admiration if they don't try to push their own world view on you. Finding a middle ground of mutual acceptance brings a peaceful energy to your relationship. There are times when you will need to be less strong-willed and more open-minded.

You came into this life to form alliances with others without endless friction. Your persistence to make a relationship a success comes from a tenacious mind. Knowing when you have done all that it is possible to keep a strong bond with a person comes with wisdom gained through experience. You might be perceived as someone not giving up on a friendship during times of adversity. Sometimes your need for stability leaves you sacrificing things in order to keep the peace.

People who are not afraid to show their passion in living their life quickly come into your awareness. It wakes up your own passion senses and stimulates your creativity. Someone paying attention to your emotional and sensual needs finds entry into your inner world. You can feel attracted to people who are different from you emotionally. Outgoing people can pull you out of your shell and ignite your need for closeness. Feeling comfortable with people relaxes your mental energies.

The Taurus Past Life Karmic Patterns

Past life memories claim a resting place in our consciousness. These energies at times weave their way into our current life. You may feel a connection with some of the Taurus past life patterns that will be discussed. If there are any that particularly strike a chord with you don't let this bother you. Each of us has past life themes that have gained entry into our current incarnation.

Think of it as a learning experience and an opportunity to make a course correction. It is your chance to gain greater insight into a past life shadow that wants you to bring it out into the healing light.

As a Taurus your consistent determination to transform the negative pull of a pattern into an empowering ally can become a reality. It does take a certain amount of practice to overcome a past life pattern. Don't get discouraged if a pattern seems to reemerge in your life no matter your effort. At some point your movement through a pattern will occur. Think of this like strengthening a muscle in your body. You are empowering your mind and inner spirit as you acknowledge a pattern is active in your life.

Low Self-Esteem
If at times you are sensing your self-esteem in a relationship has taken a downward motion it could be a trend from past incarnations. This does not mean that in all of your past lives you had low self-worth. It could be certain people have a way of awakening this pattern, causing you to feel insecure and self-conscious. This past life pattern can suddenly manifest like a shadow that feels uncomfortable or foreign to your usual way of handling your relationships with people. You could find yourself feeling confused about why certain people seem to reveal these hidden parts of yourself.

It is very possible you are attracting individuals that have a way of negating your positive energy. This can be a past life pattern operating on a subconscious level that manifests suddenly. That part of you looking for a person to support your goals is strong within you. When you are in relationships that stand in the way of your longing for mutual acceptance it is a test to hang onto your self-esteem. If you put the extra effort into these relationships and do some self-examination, things tend to work out in your favor. The important thing about this pattern is for you to see yourself clearly and to know that no one is perfect. As long as you are willing to make changes and adapt to the situation you will find peace. In the end, harmony in relationships is extremely important for you to feel comfortable.

I Need Peace

There are people who bring out our intensity. Some of them make great partners and lovers. Passion can be a beautiful thing, but if you are regularly in relationships that are sparring contests it can grow old. This past life pattern is in contradiction to the natural fondness for serenity in the soul of a Taurus. It isn't that a temporary quarrel with someone is a big problem. But if you are living in a world of extreme tension with someone, it wears down your mental and emotional energy. An argument that goes on over an extended time period with no resolution in sight causes resentment. It can also make you feel stressed and develop a need to control the other person.

Venus is the ruling planet of your Taurus slice of the zodiac pie. This planet thrives on being able to compromise. Venus wants peace and harmony. If you can't find equal territorial rights in a relationship with someone and feeling at ease is a challenge, it's time to move on. Your Taurus nature needs to know the give and take is balanced. Otherwise, you will find yourself pulling away from a person, either mentally or physically, who has become a thorn in your side and causing you great stress. You have to remember that you can't force someone to change, they have to want to.

Fixed Attitudes

Your sign has a strong endurance that can outlast many challenges that at times defies the odds. When you are determined to make a goal a success there is nothing that will stand in your way. If this pattern works its way into your relationships, that focusing power you adopt can backfire. How might this occur? Your ideas could lack flexibility which makes communication breakdowns with others a greater possibility. This past-life pattern may lie dormant, sleeping silently until you are in relationships with people that are not good at accepting change. If someone is similar to you, and equally strong-willed, it can feel like bulls locking horns. The chemistry in such a relationship can come to a grinding halt with neither of you willing to budge.

You might find that an easier, more adaptable personality suits you best. If you maintain fixed perceptions and if you are not willing to make an adjustment, this can isolate you from the closeness you seek. Another way this pattern manifests is getting into relationships with individuals with one sided ways of looking at situations. That one side is what is best for them. This does not make for much teamwork when you need a reasonable partner. If you are with someone refusing to listen to your input about serious plans that need both of your involvement, the result will disappoint you.

Lost Dreams

Each of us comes into this life with intuition that can guide us to dream of a better future. If this past life shadow energy becomes activated, it might find you too willing to please others. Your need for comfort, harmony, and peace can at times cause you to feel taken for granted. When this occurs, your passion to pursue your own unique goals could suffer a setback. If you are in a partnership where someone is constantly talking you out of pursuing a growth promoting activity you could miss out on a mentally invigorating experience. This can be a recurring pattern from past lives that has worked its way in from your memory bank. It might not even be realized by you on a conscious level that you are engaged in this pattern. It is possible you could feel as though you are in a bad dream. Especially if you feel that much of the time you let others step on your plans to make important changes in your life. That

Taurus willpower you own gets weakened if surrendered to the viewpoint of someone lacking the ability to share your need for a better today and tomorrow. You need an affectionate, supportive, and reliable partner who believes in your goals and even helps you financially to achieve them.

Possessiveness

In this past-life pattern of possessiveness, if it becomes too active it can find you becoming too bossy and even controlling. Why might this happen? It could be not trusting people due to insecurity. You might have been hurt before or there is a fear that someone will let you down. If you get attached to someone it can be difficult for you to let them go. You take relationships seriously and stubbornly want to make them work out. Certain individuals often have a way of activating this tendency from within you. Their behaviors make you feel suspicious of their actions. For example, they might be very flirtatious and fickle. It can be a fear of not being in control of situations that brings you into this past life pattern. Sometimes the very person you are attracted to also makes you feel unsettled and uncomfortable. Taurus instincts want to keep relationships stable and safe. It might be that some individuals make you feel like you must be in control.

You might get accused of being clingy, jealous, and insecure. The other side of this pattern is that you might be attracting people that are too possessive of you. It is their manipulative behavior that can have a smothering effect. You could be afraid of losing this type of person if you call them out on their behavior. It's hard for you to communicate conflict or unpleasant feelings with others, you would much rather keep the peace. This will eventually give you a feeling of being trapped in a limiting relationship. This is not saying all of your past lives were like this. It is only revealing that this is a pattern you could have brought into this incarnation to leave behind.

Clash of Values

This is a past life pattern that comes to the surface in relating to others whose values are at odds with your own. It has more to do with each of you not being able to clearly communicate a need for mutual acceptance of what is important to you. It is also caused due to traditional, judgmental, or conservative opinions you both might hold. Respecting one another's need for individual self-expression is usually at the root of this tension. In this incarnation, when you have experienced a key insight that tells you that you need to move in a new creative direction, it can cause a disruption with a partner. Your own passion to make choices that bring new growth might be perceived inaccurately by others. If you can't find the middle ground to get the freedom to be yourself a power struggle can result. This, in itself, is a natural occurrence. It can be a problem if you are expected to act like you have not had a new idea of what inspires you in life.

If you have to constantly hide your new life interests from someone it does start to wear on your energy levels. After all, you have to be you. An authentic you is what nourishes that Taurus sense of fulfillment. If you can't live out what you value, something will always feel like it is missing.

Fear of Adversity

Your Taurus nature gravitates toward seeking pleasant life experiences. You want to feel calm and grounded. That is a good thing to want in life. None of us can afford to reject feelings of inner peace and serenity. All relationships will go through some ups and downs periodically. If this past life pattern pays you a visit, you might find yourself leaving a promising partnership too early. Friction in a relationship may bombard your nervous system with too much anxiety. This doesn't mean you should stay in a relationship that is bad for your health. But if you vacate a relationship too soon, when you first experience a disagreement, you might be giving up on a potentially good thing.

If you stay with someone to work out a problem it can prove to be a valuable learning experience for each of you. You will get stronger when facing adversity in a more direct way. This pattern weakens in its intensity when you focus on positive outcomes. Don't let worries invade your sense of security. There are no perfect people which means there are no perfect relationships. If you can remember that you have flaws just as others do, admit them, and put effort into being honest with others then this pattern will be subdued. If you run away from adversity, it tends to often appear bigger than it is in reality. Face your fears and allow yourself to feel uncomfortable. Everything in life can't always be peaceful. You benefit when you learn how to handle conflict.

Stuck in the Past

This pattern, if emerging into the current incarnation, is linked to a few different possibilities, one being that you can't shake the attachment to a past relationship. You are a nostalgic person and have strong memories. If you are disappointed that a relationship ended and that you truly are still attached, then it can obstruct a new love from starting. Taurus has more stamina than most signs to keep feeling a relationship can be fixed even when a partner has left. The longing to find someone who is like a past lover can cause you to measure other people to a certain standard. This can prevent the opportunity of meeting someone new. Sometimes letting go is the only way you can move forward. Cutting ties can be painful but in the long run it can help you attract new relationships into your life.

The past can even affect you subconsciously and have you looking for a soul mate that resembles or reminds you of a past life love. This is only a problem if you want a person to live up to unreasonable expectations. No one will ever be exactly like your past life love. You may not be aware that there is a past-life love partner that is shadowing your perceptions when looking at a new potential love experience. In this instance you are not allowing the current life to unfold in a way that allows you to have fulfillment with a new individual.

Living in Shallow Water

Developing emotional depth in relating to others takes time. This is a past-life pattern that, when activated, finds you pulling back from someone to hide your feelings. Usually, a lack of trust is at the root of this pattern. It is not so unusual when a relationship is beginning not to reveal our deeper self. As the bond between two people gets stronger there is a foundation on which to build trust. It could be that someone is causing you to avoid the deeper emotional waters. If this repeats itself on an ongoing basis, swimming to the deeper end of the emotional water is a problem. You could be attracting people who cause this past life pattern to surface. Their own unwillingness to talk about their feelings could be the reason for wanting to get deeper emotionally. It could be that in some past lifetimes it was difficult to find a partner willing to open up their emotional world to you. If this keeps occurring in this lifetime when you are involved with a person for a long duration of time, you will sense that you deserve a closer emotional connection.

Cannot Live With or Without You

This past life pattern usually can be traced back along a trail of indecision on the one hand and possibly looking for too much perfection in people on the other. The lack of decisiveness about relationships might be due to a hesitation in wanting to make a commitment. Being careful and patient is a wise thing to do. But always finding a reason that all people are not the right fit for you could be due to either a fear of commitment or a feeling that there has to be a right person waiting for you to find them.

If you find that this pattern hits the mark with you, it is just possible this is a theme that followed you into this incarnation. There can be a sense or feeling that you are close to a person yet you want to distance yourself from them at the same time. This pattern can give you the sensation that you are in a constant struggle, seeking intimacy with someone and yet at the same time desiring space. Making peace with these opposites is the challenge.

Too Guarded

If this past life pattern is activated it can find you feeling too protective of yourself, blocking anyone from getting too close. You might be afraid of being vulnerable and opening up to others. It is a good idea to be sure you can trust someone before letting them into your inner world. But if you always close the door to letting someone get to know you deeply, it will make a solid relationship hard to create. It does involve risk-taking to allow for greater intimacy in your life. There is no rule that says you have to move fast into a physical relationship. This pattern reduces in intensity when you let go of your fear of letting a person form a bond with you based on trust.

Another way this pattern manifests itself is if you are inviting people into your life that are too guarded. In other words, it is a past life pattern that could take the form of encountering people that hide their true selves too much of the time. They are mirroring something you came into this life to work on and transform. Sometimes the thing each of us needs to overcome from a past life is presented to us in the people we meet. Look at it as an opportunity to see the pattern in someone else and not something you want to bring into your own life.

Boundary Confusion

Your Taurus earth sign can be very pragmatic about what you look for in friends and lovers. There is a need to keep your feet on solid ground even when falling in love. If this past life pattern is awakened in the current incarnation, your boundaries can become blurred. This could result in you not having a clear picture on how to define a relationship. You might find yourself in a state of emotional confusion when your boundaries are not clear. Your life might feel out of control, especially when strong emotions are involved. Sometimes the cause of this past life pattern is to want too much from someone, or your partner might have unrealistic expectations. Your sense of personal empowerment is less if you feel that the territory you need to be yourself has been compromised. The greater the closeness with someone, the more potential for this pattern to emerge if there is an absence of clear communication.

The Taurus Reward for Using Your Sixth Sense Intuitive Perception to Solve Karmic Patterns

When releasing a karmic pattern, it feels like a breath of wholesome fresh air has replenished your mind, body and soul. It might even give you a sense of a powerful rebirth. Your relationships have a new path to becoming fulfilling experiences. In some ways you are rewarding yourself with a new gift each time you find the determination to overcome the negative pull of a past life pattern. The shadow force when brought into the light of a new, clearer awareness is wonderful. The potential for greater harmony in your relationships becomes a reality.

If one of these karmic patterns rings true for you, it is not meant to worry you. On the contrary, hopefully you will see there are other positive ways to express these energies. Often a karmic pattern is hidden from our conscious awareness. It can take practice to get better at not letting a past life pattern interfere with the happiness you want to achieve in this lifetime. The first step is to recognize when a karmic pattern is active in your life. It is then that you will begin to hold the key to opening the door to greater self-discovery.

If the Low Self-Esteem pattern followed you into this incarnation then you need to get good at rewarding yourself with whatever it takes to get you to a higher level. It does not need to happen all at once. It will take some of that Taurus patience and persistence your sign is known to have. You will be surprised to see how quickly you can start to move in a new, positive direction if you slowly take the first steps. You will feel a renewed creative spark in believing that you deserve to bring more fulfilling experiences into your life. It is important that you remember that you deserve to feel valued and to experience closeness.

People who have negative perceptions of you do not need to occupy your mind. Perhaps you need to get tougher mentally to ward off the input from others that lowers your self-worth. This process of not accepting the negative opinions of you from others will then become a normal part of your everyday operation in the world. You did not come into this life to repeat this pattern. Develop positive thinking and an optimistic focus and you will leave this pattern behind you.

The I Need Peace pattern might only need a slight tweak in your perception to get you on a smoother road to harmony. Some intensity in life is normal and often is a catalyst to launch change. A Taurus like yourself tends to get overwhelmed when there is constant discord in your everyday life. You value being calm, relaxed, and easygoing. If you are in relationships that have little peace, it makes life seem like a struggle. Sometimes this pattern will find its way into an incarnation if you have a partner in the habit of creating a crisis. If you can stay away from people wanting to escalate drama and avoid people who like chaos, you will be happier. Seeking out people who truly want an equal and healthy partnership is one sure way to balance out this pattern. A winning formula to overcome this pattern is by surrounding yourself with individuals who want to achieve harmony rather than ones that are looking to create struggles with no understanding of how to put out a fire they started.

The Fixed Attitudes pattern is in your wheelhouse to provide a more productive energy. Taureans can stubbornly resist making changes that are true. Then again you have to get down to business energy that you can put into motion to create a new insight. If this past life pattern tries to zero in on you, the best remedy is flexibility. It is a sure way to get the communication flowing with people. You need not compromise your own goals. What is likely to be the result of showing an open mind is that you will get more support for your ideas. It is also good to admit when you are wrong or if you make a mistake. Saying sorry and listening to others does wonders for relationship satisfaction.

This pattern can mean that in some past lifetimes you had to deal with people having closed minds on a regular basis. If this is a repeat performance it can be frustrating. If individuals are always trying to interfere with your future plans by asserting their own rigid opinions, you will need to find the confidence to stay focused on your goals. The main message here is to remember to be willing to change direction and stay open to new learning. Try not to allow the negative opinions of others and the naysayers to drive the direction you want to go in.

The Lost Dreams pattern, if it becomes too active in your current life, can be overcome in more than one way. The first thing to remember is that your sign was gifted at birth with a great amount of patience. It might feel at times that you have to outlast the influence of this past life pattern by maintaining a forward momentum to reach a goal. Having dreams of a better tomorrow is something to be cherished. You would need to express your intention to make a dream come true with greater force. This may require you to learn not to let outside opinions distract you away from what you want to accomplish.

Often it is our intuition that shows us how to have a dream to reach out to and that guides us to make it come true. When you are in those moments of doubt, don't despair. That dream or goal giving you inspiring confidence to walk your walk is never far away. You can't always please others, which can take you away from your most heartfelt dreams. You need to put yourself first, even if it feels uncomfortable to do.

Believing in your ability is a big part of the path in letting the universe make your dreams come true.

The Possessiveness past life pattern orbits around trust issues. You need to give others the same amount of freedom you want for yourself in relationships. This pays great dividends in terms of feeling that you have a bond with someone based on trust. If you grow overly possessive of someone, it takes energy from you that could be more productively expressed. Having the confidence to let go of a need to be possessive is a liberating experience. The love and closeness you desire flourishes when you transcend this pattern.

If you attract people who have strong controlling tendencies, it requires you to stand your ground. There is a possibility that you will need to distance yourself from people with extreme possessive-like behaviors. A relationship colored with shared power is the road to personal fulfillment. When you see you don't need to tolerate individuals who don't respect your independence you are gaining the insight needed to make this past life pattern transform.

The Clash of Values past life pattern usually requires clear communication with lovers, friends and family members. Sometimes to keep the peace, the wise policy is to agree to disagree. Having ways you and a partner perceive the world independently stimulates growth for each of you. The exchange of knowledge from different points of view can be mentally stimulating. A mutual respect for each other's values builds trust. When you do come together on a shared plan it will have that much more power behind it.

What you value in life cannot be compromised if it is an important belief system that fills you with inspiration. There can be new insights that could rock the boat in a relationship. How you introduce and explain your new thinking is important to ensure it is well received. Timing is important when revealing new ideas to others and is something else to keep in mind. There may be a person who might try to talk you out of a new life direction you choose to walk. If it is a goal you greatly value, there is no price worth not pursuing it. You have to value your intuition and trust yourself. If this pattern has occurred in this lifetime, it has likely been a part of your past life history. Your Taurus personal empowerment is linked to what you value in life. It is as essential as the air you breathe.

The Fear of Adversity pattern could awaken in you that in some past lives there are some memories embedded in your consciousness reminding you of struggles in relationships. Love and passion can, at times, bring out a certain amount of intensity in a relationship. Your Taurus natural tendency is to seek tranquility in all aspects of your everyday life. If you are in a relationship that you like and learn to flow with the ups and downs, then the bond can grow stronger. People tend to need one another more when facing challenges together.

This pattern might come to the surface when you fear an argument will cause you to lose a partner. There are times it is good to bring an issue you have with another person out into the open. What appears to be a problem brings you closer together through clear communication. Your relationships can go through a rebirth by taking on adversity in a direct manner. Your ruling planet is Venus which gives you the capacity to be diplomatic when tackling a relationship issue. In finding the courage to stay in a relationship when the going gets tough, it can bring you a sense of empowerment. The milestones you can celebrate with the right partner are worth the time spent walking through the challenges together. You will become more committed, dedicated, and loyal from these intense experiences.

This Stuck in the Past pattern does not need to keep you from exploring new relationships. The past can be a great teacher that offers us wisdom. It can guide us to learn from our mistakes, so we don't repeat them. But you do need to be careful not to let it rule your thinking or prevent you from making needed changes. If you allow yourself the freedom to release the connection of a past relationship partner, it can open the door to finding someone new who will be a better fit for what you need in the present. That same Taurus energy that has been focused too much in the rear-view mirror only needs to be aimed in a forward direction.

You have to buy into the reality that you deserve people in your life that reflect who you are and want to become. It takes some courage to move ahead, even if part of you is still looking back. The reward is much greater if you close the door on the past. You came into this life to form fulfilling partnerships. The Taurus craving for love and intimacy is within your grasp when relinquishing the past.

When you feel safe in relationships with people, this Living in Shallow Water past life pattern is less likely to get activated. You may have sensed early on in your life that individuals you trust are the ones to whom you reveal your deepest feelings. You are happier on every level when being in the company of people who feel free to share their own inner world. There will always be some individuals that make us feel cautious before ever trusting them. This is actually a wise way to operate.

If you stay clear of getting too close to people who never talk about their emotions it could be a wise policy. Trying to form a deeper bond with these individuals is difficult if they insist on staying in the shallow water. If it is greater depth from a person that you want, then not settling for less is the more expansive path to personal happiness, love and harmony.

Feeling comfortable in a relationship does often require some time. The Cannot Live With or Without You pattern will test your patience in determining if you are in the right relationship for you. There is no need for guilt if you decide not to remain in a love or friendship type of relationship. This past life pattern, if activated, can be overcome. It can create some anxiety as you release the pull of this shadowy energy. If you are with someone that seems to cause you indecision, it will take your objectivity to do what is in your best interests. Passion is a wonderful thing, but obsession with a person actually takes away your power. If you make peace with this past life pattern, your sense of inner peace is the reward.

Looking for perfection in yourself or someone else can be frustrating. You will be happier when in relationships that give you a feeling of stability. A Taurus like yourself likely wants to know a partner is working as hard as you are in creating a fulfilling relationship. You will not be as happy if you are always wondering if you made the right decision in staying or leaving a relationship. Listen to that inner voice trying to guide you, to choose people who give you a reassured feeling that they want to be a trusting and loving partner. It is then you will know you have chosen the right path forward.

The Too Guarded pattern usually means you are too protective of yourself. Scrutinizing others before letting them get close is a wise thing to do, but if you always keep a barrier around you there is a chance you will miss out on a good relationship. Sometimes it is the past emotional pain endured from this life or past lives that can keep you putting out a stiff arm in the face of people. At some point in time taking the risk in letting an individual come into your world can be the first step in rising above this pattern. You don't have to reveal your inner world quickly. A Taurus likes to move at a calm and steady pace into new experiences. When you open yourself to letting down your guard, a bond with a special someone can become a reality.

If you seem to attract people who keep their guard up it might be the universe trying to give you a glimpse of how this pattern can keep you from the happiness you desire. The key thing to remember is that this current incarnation does not require you to repeat this pattern yourself. When you find that balance between your need to guard your private world and comfortably sharing intimacy, you will never have to worry about this pattern.

The Boundary Confusion pattern shows that romantic love has a particular way of blurring the boundaries with a lover. Any relationship that stirs up emotional intensity can challenge you to keep your territorial lines clearly defined. There is nothing wrong with being extra supportive when called upon for lovers, friends and family members. If this past life pattern has presented itself as a problem, then you do need to begin to balance dependency needs. You will feel more empowered when getting a handle on this pattern. Your relationships will feel more rewarding.

People in your life without their own clear boundaries benefit from your own assertiveness to claim your space. As you grow comfortable with traveling in your own lane, it has a secondary impact in showing someone else their own lane. There is a pretty good chance that your creative vitality and mental energy will be recharged when you rise above this pattern.

The Taurus Reward from Solving Karmic Patterns
Patience and determination color your Taurus Sun sign with the right stuff to deal positively with karmic patterns. The path through any past life pattern does have some challenges. If it looks like a tall mountain to climb, don't get discouraged. The relationship fulfillment you can claim when rising above a karmic pattern is a wonderful reward.

Each of us has some karmic patterns that came with us into this lifetime. You are not alone when it comes to becoming aware of a pattern and the need to deal with it. It is amazing the new energy you will feel when healing any of these patterns. It might even surprise you how your new insights help you in all areas of your life.

The way you relate to others gets an energized boost through healing a past life pattern. A brave new world awaits you when walking paths that promise new growth. Your vision will become empowered with an attitude filled with a magical self-confidence as you harmonize your understanding of a past life pattern.

Taurus the Real Person Journal Prompts

1. How do you feel when you see the Taurus image?
2. What Taurus archetype traits do you resonate with?
3. How can you be more flexible and adapt to change?
4. How can you let go of the past?
5. What things bring you comfort?
6. What are ways you express affection?
7. What past life patterns have you experienced?

Chapter Three

Gemini the Jester or Comedian

"I THINK"
Keywords: Talkative, Intellectual, Sarcastic, Friendly, Sociable, Adaptable, Restless
Sun Sign Dates: May 21–June 21
Temperament: Sanguine
Sign Type: Air, Mutable
Planetary Ruler: Mercury
Jungian Archetype: The Jester (Comedian)
Tarot Card: The Lovers
Polar Opposite Archetype: The Explorer
Astrology Nickname: The Communicator
Polar Opposite Sign: Sagittarius
Symbol: The Twins
Personality Color: Green, Extroverted
Rules: The Third House; Lungs, Hands

Temperament: Sanguine

Gemini is the third sign of the zodiac. You are the social butterfly, friendly, talkative and extroverted. Connecting with others and sharing ideas brings happiness often. The life of the party, you are fun to be around and it's difficult for others not to like you. Having mental stimulation is crucial or else you get bored. Restless at heart, the need to be moving can impact every area of your life. It is hard for you to commit to something because your energy can quickly change. Your sharp intellect makes it critical to have inspiring conversations with others. The fastest way to your heart is through exciting communication.

Being adaptable to new situations helps you make many friends. In fact, friendship is often more important to you than love. You fall in love with people and start relationships with people who start out as your friend. Indecision can cause you problems because you find it hard to choose. You often ask others what they think, but it's hard for you to actually take their advice. Talking things out, over-analyzing, and venting relieve stress. It's important to remember that there are times when other people's ideas can help you. You are optimistic, energetic, flirtatious, and witty. As a Gemini you seek knowledge, information, and enjoy making people laugh.

Gemini is associated with the sanguine temperament and is known to be quick, sarcastic, flirtatious, and outgoing. Sanguine people are warmhearted, lively, and spontaneous. You appreciate communication and networking with new people. You make friends easily but can find it challenging to commit to just one person. Having choices is important to you and fulfills your need for autonomy. Freedom and independence help you reach your goals. Sanguine personality types have a natural teaching ability and make excellent speakers. As a freedom seeker you dislike having to wait around for others and get restless if you feel withheld for any reason. Movement is important for your overall emotional well-being. Others might perceive you as restless, and always on the go, darting around talking, and making things happen.

You respond quickly and live in the moment. Your adaptability helps you adjust to stressful people and situations. Sometimes fickle, other people might feel they can't rely on you. It just takes time for you to finish projects, and you prefer to multitask and do many things at once. You prefer to live in your head and use your mind to solve problems. Avoiding responsibilities can sometimes get you in trouble. Sometimes disorganized, you can find it hard to finish things.

Jungian Archetype: Jester, Comedian

Gemini is associated with the Jester archetype. You are an electric and changeable personality. You attract friends instantly because of your carefree and playful persona. It's hard not to feel connected to you instantly. As a jester or comedian, you have the ability to make people laugh with your witty and sarcastic comments. Just like the Jester, Geminis don't take things too seriously and sometimes struggle with commitment. You need variety in your life, or you grow bored. Having people to spend time socializing with brings happiness. There is an air of spontaneity that makes others feel you are free-spirited and exciting. If you feel tied down or controlled, you will rebel and need to roam. No one can hold you back if you have a new idea or thought to pursue. Short journeys and socializing during your travels can help you accumulate knowledge. Telling the truth in a fun, light-hearted way often makes other people feel at ease. You can feel great joy from seeing others giggle and laugh at a joke you tell. You like to entertain others and love verbal duals. Sometimes you try to lighten a heavy room or if people are brooding or negative you will try to shock them with a quip. You like to remind other people not to take the world too seriously.

Tarot Card Archetype: The Lovers

The Lovers card in the tarot deck is associated with the Gemini archetype. In astrology, Gemini is associated with twins. This card is about meaningful connections. Socializing, flirting, and talking is what you do best. In this image, you see both a male and female, representing duality. This also represents the two sides of your nature. Many people believe that Geminis have two distinct personalities. You have a hidden side often associated with shadow energy. One side of you can be friendly, fun, and happy and then the other can be moody, irritable, and cutting with your words. You will always struggle to choose one thing and want to have many options. Geminis, just like the Lover's archetype, enjoy being curious and establishing intellectual connections. Having the freedom of choice, and ability to learn, communicate and explore many different relationships helps you find fulfillment.

Geminis, like the Lovers, often get confused by making decisions. This is why there is both a male and female portrayed in this card. You might like to keep your options open and not commit to one path. The essence of duality is how you function in many areas of your life. Being limited in your decisions can feel stifling and force you to move on impulsively. Cutting ties is easy when you feel controlled, possessed, or trapped. It's best to always weigh both options thoroughly. The greatest lesson for a Gemini is to learn to balance thoughts and emotions. You enjoy having more than one option.

Sign Type: Air Element

Gemini is an air sign which makes you intelligent, social, and communicative. Because you are an air sign, you feel a need for freedom and independence. Having autonomy and a multitude of interests keeps your mind active. You are often restless, changeable, and spontaneous. Accomplishing mental tasks and learning new things is important to you. Happiness often comes through educational achievement and pushing yourself to face mental challenges. Traditional schooling can be difficult, and you often prefer to learn on your own. Teaching yourself comes easily and you have a powerful memory. You like to be creative, inspiring, and innovative in everything you do. There is a good chance you are a natural speaker and teacher. Explaining things on a basic level comes naturally for you. Anything mundane or too practical is boring and can cause restlessness. Mental challenges awaken your curiosity. There is a deep need for communication and discussion with friends, co-workers, and loved ones. You have a knack for networking and gaining many acquaintances. People like you because you are funny and can make them laugh during difficult times. There is a friendliness about you but also a detached emotional side. Accumulating knowledge through travel, classes, and studying on your own is where you thrive.

Personality Color: Green

Gemini is the essence of the color green. You are intellectual, rebellious, freedom-loving, and educated. You dislike order, predictability, and rules. There is a desire to break free of tradition and question authority. Anything or anyone who lacks intelligence or knowledge irritates you. Creative minds and people who can carry on a good conversation comfort your restless nature.

In fact, you are always looking for new and exciting ways to do things. Highly changeable, adaptable, and restless it's hard for you to be relied upon. Other people might feel like you are unstable or sometimes untruthful. You get bored easily with basic tasks and responsibilities. As a green personality you need a mental challenge in order to get motivated to do your work. You get along best with other green personalities, namely the other air signs, Libra and Aquarius. You like things to happen quickly and can make decisions abruptly. You can think on your feet but can sometimes overthink, obsess, and over-analyze decisions. Then the next minute you can completely change your mind and want to do something different. Other people have a hard time keeping up with your quick and agile mind. Change is something you appreciate and adapt to quite easily. You are a high-energy person who enjoys communication, learning, partying, flirting, and having fun.

The Gemini Current Life Relationship Landscape

If you were born under the sign of Gemini, you came into this life to relate to a wide variety of people. In fact, your curiosity drives you to explore the minds of others. Sharing ideas with a lover, friend, business associate, or family member is a stimulating experience. Being in relationships with an individual who likes to openly share what is on their mind appeals to you. Those who hide their thoughts from you on a continual basis can worry you. You can feel uncomfortable around people who don't communicate well. Connecting to others comes through communication. Your energetic way of wanting to seek new ideas and learning attracts people to you.

Travel on the mental and physical levels is in your sign's DNA. There is a desire to find people who are open to the way you perceive the world around you. A person does not have to agree with all of your ideas; you only want to know that they are listening to you.

There are times you will need to change a life direction quickly. Your mind lives in the moment and your closest allies in life really like that about you. You could grow frustrated with people who try to limit your options. The more roads to success and happiness in your imagination, the more fulfilled you feel. It's important for you to feel you have many options.

Your mind tends to work fast. Individuals who connect with this part of you seem to understand you. You want to be accepted as a freethinker. Being open-minded and accepting of different views is important. Even though you're friendly, some might find you aloof. You like to think of this as being in the process of mentally processing life as it is happening. Being free and adaptable are your strengths. You need people in your life who understand your need for change and flexibility.

The Gemini Past Life Karmic Patterns

Past life memories are helpful if you see them as learning experiences. Every sign has brought something from past incarnations into this lifetime to balance. The information in this book is meant to serve as a guide to help you integrate a past life pattern into the current life in a more harmonious way. In gaining awareness of a past life pattern, it starts the process of a new self-discovery.

As a Gemini, your piercing intellect can navigate through any past life pattern with new insight. It can take some practice in finding the inner strength to keep moving in a clearer direction regarding a past life pattern. The patterns being discussed lessen in their influence when you gain the confidence to transform them into illuminating energies. Remember to enjoy the journey in rising above a past life pattern, as this is the lighthouse that will always be there for you.

If you recognize any of the karmic patterns as having been encountered in this incarnation, the key is to look at it as a learning experience. You will gain greater confidence in dealing with a pattern as you learn how to not let it interfere with the happiness you want in your relationships. Be patient. Chances are it will take some time to more productively channel a karmic pattern in a new positive direction. It could help you attract people to you that want to establish a fulfilling partnership. Remember to acknowledge that a pattern is the beginning of a walk on a new path by allowing stimulating insights that can make the journey one that brings personal and relationship fulfillment.

Hiding Behind the Intellect

If this past life pattern becomes an active part in how you relate to others, then your intellect could conceal your emotions in relationships too much of the time. As a Gemini, your first impulse is to think and focus on your mind. This is your primary way of connecting with people. In your closest relationships, your mental side could become a problem if it will not allow your feelings to be expressed. There are times you may not even realize you are doing this. There can be occasions when a pattern has become activated, and it acts like it is a natural part of your thought processes. A lover, friend or family member may perceive you are distancing yourself purposely. It is not unusual when first entering a new relationship to not reveal your innermost world. But as time goes on, if you are not willing to communicate your feelings, then it could cause a lack of trust in how you relate to others. As an air sign, Gemini has a greater reliance on the mental side of life. Crossing over into feelings can be a challenge. If you never risk being honest about your emotions and feelings, it could make closeness difficult to achieve with others.

In the Hiding Behind the Intellect past life pattern, it does not take a big tweak to solve the challenge of sharing more of your feelings. It is better for your overall mental and emotional balance to let those you want to bring closer have access to your inner world. Passion with a lover deepens when you open up about your emotional depth. Trust develops through taking the risk of allowing someone to get a clear picture of your emotions. You don't have to reveal all of your secrets. The important thing is that you communicate and build deeper connections with others. Greater intimacy in your relationships is the reward for working your way through this pattern. Your communication skills are powerful and a tremendous asset. Your perceptions about people you feel comfortable are a bridge to allowing you to express your feelings. Taking that first step in letting someone see the inner you is the path to releasing this pattern. That means staying invested and interested in taking time to truly get to know others on a deeper level.

Mixed Signals

This pattern, if emerging in your life, can have more than one cause. One way it can manifest itself is through self-doubt. It causes a lack of decisiveness and can interfere in having clear communication with others. It can make having a commitment with someone a real challenge. Another path this pattern can take is purposely giving misleading information to others. It does make giving a clear picture of what you need from someone confusing. It will feel like you are going around in cloudy circles in defining a relationship clearly. If you continue going down this road it can keep you from having relationship fulfillment. If you are wanting support for your goals from others it may not be there when you need it most.

The Mixed Signals pattern could be linked to past incarnations where you were in relationships that lacked clear definition. It does not mean all of your past lives were like this. To avoid a repeat performance in acting out this pattern you only need to give clear messages to others. The support for your goals becomes strengthened when you communicate what you need from others clearly. You might have some self-doubt or don't feel deserving of a solid relationship. If you can move into a more positive frame of mind this pattern will disappear.

It is possible that you are in relationships that feature this pattern, meaning it is a partner with this influence. It is your chance to recognize this is happening and have your own insight, being clear that you don't want to go back into this pattern yourself. Being able to identify this pattern in others is your ticket out of this past life energy.

Yo-Yo

This pattern, if activated in your life, is acted out by making someone feel close and then suddenly pushing them away. It could be an unpredictable behavior that unexpectedly takes place. You could be surprised yourself when this occurs. A past life pattern can hang around in the background of our conscious awareness. Then when a situation presents itself, like you are not sure just how close you want to be with someone, this pattern comes quickly into being. What causes this? It is possible you don't yet trust that a relationship is really what you need at the present time. This pattern is a problem if you feel you have met someone special but can't seem to stop this pattern from getting in the way of your happiness. Your mind does work fast and may at times jump to conclusions that a relationship is moving at a quicker pace than you find comfortable. There is nothing wrong with this reasoning. But if this is an ongoing and regular event in your life, it is likely this pattern is interfering in a way that could be limiting your chances for relationship harmony.

The Yo-Yo pattern can be overcome if you don't distance yourself from someone without warning. There is nothing wrong with wanting some space if needed. If you give advance warning when you need time alone, it lessens the interference of this pattern. You will find it is possible to have closeness and distance as required if you take the time to communicate clearly. Chances are if you have the right people in your life they will also want some time to themselves to pursue their own goals. It is not unusual for Gemini individuals to need a certain amount of free time. You probably have multiple ideas to pursue that may take you away for periods of time from those you love and cherish. It is not that difficult to keep someone close. Let them know they are important even when you are apart. Stay supportive of the goals of a friend or lover and the intimacy is always present.

Emotional Burnout

This past life pattern for a Gemini like yourself usually will make its entrance if you have an ongoing rollercoaster ride of emotions in a relationship. Emotional turmoil with someone you care about begins to wear on your mental strength. If you can't find emotional stability in a relationship, it is painful. This could be a leftover pattern from some past lives where you could not find the inner peace you so badly needed. You don't have to repeat the pattern. But if you stay emotionally confused it makes for not much fun in how you relate to others.

It could be you find yourself in a relationship with a person that tends to push your emotional buttons quickly. If you stay in relationships that lack clear communication, this pattern has a bigger opportunity to emerge into your life. Your intuition may feel stifled in relationships that require too much of you, especially giving too much emotional support and not receiving enough in return. If the dependency needs get out of balance, you will sense something you need for fulfillment is missing.

The Emotional Burnout pattern can be navigated around if you remain vigilant about not letting it into your life. The more you insist on people working with you rather than against you, the more likely this past life shadow will disappear from your life. It is easier to tune into your intuition when your emotions are in balance. You have a strong mental nature being a Gemini. Your insights stay sharper when your emotional energy remains strong. There are going to be times when you and the important people in your life will be at odds over certain plans you have. This is only a problem if those differences begin to put a great strain on the relationship. Dependency needs with an equal give and take maintains the peace. With practice you can sense when emotional tension between you and others has reached too high a level. It helps to stay centered and grounded through taking walks, meditation and whatever techniques you find that keep you happy and healthy.

Keeping You Guessing

This pattern is aggravating if it comes into play. When someone is hiding what they really want from you, it can create much anxiety in your life. Honest communication may be too absent. Gemini people don't mind surprises as it keeps life interesting; being deceived by an individual's intentions is a whole other story. If you are trying to get close to someone but sense a wall around them, it does make it difficult to establish trust. It can grow frustrating, trying to figure someone out as time goes on. It will test your patience probably more than you want if a person will not reveal what they want from you. The mystique and intrigue of meeting someone new can be exciting. But it wears thin if it stays at that level over a long time period. Intimacy could be out of reach, which can be disappointing if you stay stuck in this pattern. This could be a repeating past life influence where you get involved with people purposely misleading you.

The Keeping You Guessing past life pattern wastes too much energy if you can't get someone to reveal their expectations of you and what they really are looking for in a relationship. It is far better to let someone know how this is impacting you. If this pattern has been repeating, you probably need to be more assertive in getting a relationship to move faster in the direction you prefer. Sometimes this has more to do with a partner, who may be reluctant, for whatever reason, to make a commitment or at least give a clearer definition of the relationship. You are better off in having a standard that will not allow for ongoing communication confusion. The more emotionally intense a relationship is, is perhaps a time where you need to wear your business hat and find out quicker what your partner's goal is for you being together. It may come down to telling yourself that a reality check is needed to get a clearer vision of how you fit into the relationship.

Hidden Anger

A Gemini cannot hold back anger for extended periods without it eventually exploding right in front of you. It might even surprise you to see it all come out at once. You and all of the people that are important to you are better off if you express your ideas in the moment. It is true some friction can result if you are direct with others. Your relationships do get empowered if you are openly assertive. Diplomacy can be woven into sensitive subjects. If you associate with friends and lovers who want you to tiptoe around them, it probably won't last for long. Eventually you need to say what is on your mind. If you keep swallowing anger, it gets bigger and bigger inside of you and is rough on your nervous system. Your verbal skills as a Gemini need to be displayed. If you are in a relationship with someone causing you to deny your angry feelings over and over, this becomes problematic.

The Hidden Anger past life pattern has to be dealt with if it comes onto your current life scene. The Gemini nervous system is much better off when you make your ideas known in the moment. Anger is a raw emotion. You are an air sign which features an intellect that stays clear when not holding back anger for extended time periods. Sometimes the fear of letting anger out is worse than trying to hide it. If you become good at not holding resentment towards someone after stuffing down hurt feelings, your mental perceptions stay clear. You will have much more creative energy lined with a positive outlook when not giving into this pattern. Your relationships become empowered and might even go through a rebirth when you ascend to higher ground in releasing this past life influence.

Endless Boredom
Every relationship needs some routines to stay grounded and maintain a sense of direction. One thing that can derail a relationship for a Gemini is boredom. You need people in your life that are adaptable and don't fear change. Or at least you require a partner that gives you the freedom to keep your mind stimulated. Variety is the spice of life is a mantra never too far from the Gemini mind. Exploring new ideas and areas of interest together with a lover keeps the relationship growing. If you remain in relationships that grow stale this pattern will weave its way into your life. You will possibly become extremely restless and begin to doubt if your relationship can sustain your need for more vibrancy. Past lives when this karmic shadow

presented itself found you feeling the urge to go where the grass seemed greener.

The Endless Boredom pattern seems counterintuitive in every way for a Gemini. Relationships require people who to some degree keep you mentally stimulated. Otherwise, storm clouds of inner restlessness circulate through your mind. If you are in a relationship with a stable partner who might have different life interests, you need the freedom to pursue activities that give you a sense of growth. If your friends and lovers share your desire for exploring new learning you feel on top of the world. The key thing to remember to keep this pattern in check is to not let boredom be a frequent companion. When you are feeding your mind invigorating experiences, your relationships get an intimacy as well as a passion recharge.

Looking for the Negative

If this pattern gains too much access to your thinking there is a tendency to find fault with people even if there are no real problems. You do have an analytical tendency that can look for perfection that could be impossible for someone to fulfill. It may be that you put yourself under a microscope too often that causes a disruption in your relationships because you demand too much from yourself. If you lose sight of positive thinking, it does tend to make finding harmony with others difficult to reach. Your mind will create problems that sabotage the happiness you want to have if this pattern becomes too much of a companion.

Another way this past life pattern can surface is by being in relationships with people who display this pattern. If you deny this is occurring you will continue to attract this type of person into your life. Sometimes this happens when you don't trust your insights. You may catch glimpses that a person is lost in negativity but refuse to confront your partner. This could be a past life pattern you have come into this life to transcend. You are getting an opportunity to see firsthand that this is a pattern you want to keep at a great distance.

The Looking for the Negative pattern presents a challenge you are fully equipped to handle. When you trust your insights, it does put you in the driver's seat in putting this pattern in the rear-view mirror. You are blessed with a powerhouse of a Gemini mind. You might need to dial back an intense search for perfection in yourself or others. Training your mind to think positively, if needed, comes with practice. When you see the cup at least half full your relationships flow better. There is nothing like positive reinforcement to elevate your mind above the hold of this pattern.

If you are in relationships with those who tend to have a negative outlook much of the time, it does weigh on your energy. If you don't deny you perceive this in others it helps you to create clarity in your relationships. It might even help a partner be happier if you engage the negative tendency in their thought processes. In reaching out for the positive energy in other people, your relationships travel a path to harmony and fulfillment.

False Assumptions

The Gemini mind can move at great speed. If this past life pattern gets activated as a dominant force you could come to wrong conclusions about people. You could lose your objectivity by not taking the time to step away from situations. By focusing excessively on what could go wrong, it could cause this to occur. It is possible you keep expecting someone to fall back into behaviors you asked them to stop. Often it is emotional confusion which can cloud your mental perceptions to be the cause of this pattern. You have a great capacity to find your way out of this pattern. But if your mind gets caught up in assuming people will not be able to act in the ways you need them to perform, your relationships will fall short of your hope for fulfillment.

The False Assumptions pattern only requires you to go a little slower before making a final judgment about people. There are going to be occasions that your first perception will be very accurate. But a relationship that will stand the test of time might ask you to be patient. The first impressions of others may only be part of their persona or personal style. It is likely not revealing their deeper dimensions of who they choose to show you in the beginning. You have a mind that travels along fast brain circuitry. It only needs to go at a slower pace or give a relationship a closer look before jumping to conclusions. If you recognize this as a past life pattern active in the present incarnation it can be overcome by learning to be a good listener. Taking the time to participate in real communication with someone is the road to finding a true soul mate.

Over Worrying

There is attention to detail in Mercury-ruled signs like Gemini. If it becomes too obsessive in worrying about the little things, it can aggravate you in your relationships. This is a pattern that may not be obvious you are even caught up in it. If you maintain a vision of what you like in a relationship in a reasonable way this pattern lessens in its intensity. If you are spending too much of the time thinking about how to create a perfect partnership or friendship, it eats away at your happiness. There is divine discontent at the root of this past life influence. This means it is a difficult challenge to accept that each of us has some faults. There is no perfect soul mate in the world. Working through problems is part of the deal. Accepting this is not easy if this pattern gets too active in your life.

The Over Worrying pattern only needs you to channel your energy in more positive directions. If this sounds too difficult to accomplish it really isn't. You have one of the most adaptable of the twelve astrological signs. This is quite an asset when dealing with past life influences. You are happier and have greater vitality to enjoy your relationships when worry is kept to a minimum. Expecting perfection from yourself or others is not possible to attain. The big reward when rising above this pattern is being able to attract a great companionship with someone. You will feel mentally invigorated and will enjoy the intimacy you seek with a person when putting excess worry away from you.

Communication Breakdown

There probably is nothing worse for a Gemini like yourself to experience than a serious communication breakdown in a relationship. This is a pattern that occurs when you are in a relationship with someone and a wall appears between the two of you. Usually this happens if you and a partner have stopped hearing what the other is saying. It is as if you are both speaking in a foreign language. It can be hurtful if you sense someone has stopped truly listening to you. Sometimes this pattern comes into being if you lose your patience with others.

You might encounter this pattern when in a relationship with a person who cuts off communication at the slightest sign of a disagreement. It might be you are getting a chance to see the pattern as an opportunity to recognize a theme you no longer choose to adopt for yourself. Sometimes a past life pattern will present itself in the behavior of a person we are trying to get to understand better. If you engage in the same way of acting out this pattern you will not find the harmony you seek.

Too much silence in a relationship does not usually work for a Gemini. The Communication Breakdown pattern feels like there is too much distance between you and the other person. Finding the way back to peace, friendship and love is closer than you might think. Listening to each other's mutual need to be heard is the first step. The passion and emotional support you desire could be faster to accomplish if some compromise is reached. There can be emotional intensity over hurt feelings causing the lack of talking things out. If you take the time to pause, you probably will gain a more objective view of situations. Your mind travels fast and there will be times that slowing down your reaction time can help to resolve differences.

This pattern can present itself through people you know. The universe can work this way to give each of us a chance to get a view of how a pattern can manifest. The key thing here is that you are able to perceive this is a behavior you no longer want to wear yourself. When you speak from your heart and show your feelings, your words make others want to connect with you in magical ways.

Too Much Criticism

Criticism is a delicate subject in most relationships. As a past life pattern, it can creep in when you least expect it. This pattern can drive a deep wedge between you and others if it is overused. If it becomes a tool to hurt those you love, it becomes a very negative energy that drives people away. Tension becomes the norm rather than a closer form of intimacy if criticism gets out of control. There are times you have to accept your differences with someone to keep the peace.

If you happen to be the person receiving the brunt of criticism it could hit a nerve in you. Why? It may be a past life pattern that you came into to this life to not overindulge in using. An individual regularly critical of your decisions could be pushing a past life memory button within your consciousness. If you fail to confront the individual, it can be a real drain on your energy.

The Too Much Criticism pattern is easier to transform if you look for the positive in others first. There will be times when you will not be happy with the actions of someone you love and will feel the need to point out what bothers you. This is normal. If you can let some things go and realize that nobody is perfect, then you will find this past life energy gets quieter. If the goal is to find harmony and love with someone and you keep that as the central focus, this pattern has a tendency to leave you alone. There is often an intense energy behind this pattern that when directed toward creative pursuits and goals will bring great success. In other words, you are directing the energy to go along paths that are rewarding. It takes the pressure off the relationship.

If it is true that you are in relationships with overly critical people as a repeating event, you are better off breaking the cycle, either by making it known you need more positive energy from people or avoiding this type of person in your life. A past life pattern can occur in the form of someone using this type of behavior. It is an opportunity to recognize this pattern in someone else and do your best to get out of its presence.

Gemini Paths to Transforming
Karmic Relationship Patterns

A Gemini needs to know there are options to letting go of any karmic pattern. This is a key ingredient to your ability to gain the insight to get a pattern to release its grip on you. The freedom you will feel in facing a past life shadow energy will energize your mind in empowering ways. Your creative energy will seem like it has been given a turbo boost. Your relationships could find clearer communication and greater intimacy. Rising above a karmic past life pattern starts with small steps forward. Don't worry if you feel like you have taken a step backward. Your consistent effort to master a past life pattern will eventually pay dividends.

The Gemini Reward for Using Your Sixth Sense
Intuitive Perception to Solve Karmic Patterns

You are blessed with a mental strength that can guide you to navigate through any past life pattern. Your adaptability is a gift to step back patiently and gain a new awareness, whether you are first becoming aware of a past life pattern or working your way through one. A karmic shadow comes into the light and brings a renewed sense of yourself as you gain a new understanding of this energy. It soon becomes a reality that a past life pattern has no control over you. Your relationships find greater intimacy in releasing the hold of a pattern.

Don't worry if you connected with any of the patterns discussed. The first step in moving past a karmic energy is recognizing it; this helps give you the insight to turn the pattern into a more positive expression. Eventually, from being a frequent flyer in a pattern you begin to develop fewer urges to use it.

Your personal happiness is accelerated by rising above a past life pattern. Your goals in life get brighter and your dreams get recharged. The love you want to share gets revitalized. Your relationships become enriched with an empowered wisdom that attracts the best life has to offer you.

Gemini The Jester or Comedian Journal Prompts

1. How do you feel when you see the Gemini image?
2. What Gemini archetype traits do you resonate most with?
3. Are you a good communicator?
4. What are some new things you want to learn?
5. Where would you like to travel?
6. How can you balance your restless nature?
7. What past life patterns have you experienced?

Chapter Four

Cancer the Caregiver

"I FEEL"
Keywords: Nurturing, Sensitive, Intuitive, Mothering, Protective, Controlling, Moody
Sun Sign Dates: June 22–July 21
Temperament: Phlegmatic
Sign Type: Water, Cardinal
Planetary Ruler: Moon
Jungian Archetype: The Caregiver
Tarot Card: The Chariot
Polar Opposite Archetype: The Ruler
Astrology Nickname: The Mother
Polar Opposite Sign: Capricorn
Symbol: The Crab
Personality Color: Blue, introverted
Rules: The Fourth House; Stomach, Breasts

Temperament: Phlegmatic

Cancer is the fourth sign of the zodiac. You are a caring, kind, and sensitive soul. Taking care of others brings you a sense of fulfillment. You are attached to your home and family. It's important for you to feel comfortable and emotionally balanced. Cancers are similar to the phlegmatic personality. You are intuitive, affectionate, accepting and a wonderful listener. Phlegmatic personalities are sensitive to other people's emotions. You have a way of knowing what to say to help others feel better. Having a quiet and calm environment is crucial for your mental, emotional, and spiritual well-being. Cancer personalities are attached to the home because it's where they feel comfortable and safe. You are a mothering sign; you are nurturing to all who cross your path. At first glance you may seem private, serious, and unemotional. It can take a while for you to open up to others and be vulnerable. This is because Cancerians hide their feelings; you are deeply sensitive and get hurt easily. Because you are a phlegmatic sign, you are actually very caring and concerned about the welfare of others. You will benefit when you learn to learn to trust others and loosen your grip on them. Making time to withdraw from social situations and spending time alone in solitude are important for self-care. Having a shell protects your tender, caring, and soft interior.

Jungian Archetype: Caretaker

Cancer is the embodiment of the Caretaker archetype. You enjoy giving emotional support to others, and protecting children and animals comes naturally. Instinctive and deeply psychic, you can predict the future. Your intuition is off the charts. Having security and feeling safe is critical for your happiness. You don't want to struggle, and this is one reason you enjoy managing finances or helping others who are having a hard time. Prioritizing home and family help ground you. As a caretaker personality type you have to be careful not to overprotect or smother people. This behavior can make others feel like children or that you don't trust them. Protecting loved ones is your primary goal. But let others be responsible for their own lives and decisions. There are times you can hold on too tightly to the past and struggle to forgive. It's important to take care of your own needs and not neglect them for others. Balancing your emotions is the key when it comes to finding stability.

Tarot Card Archetype: The Chariot

The Chariot card in the tarot deck is associated with the Cancer archetype. In astrology, Cancer is known for emotional strength and protection. This card's symbolism is about balancing both the light and dark side of your personality. Determined, you have a strong willpower that helps you succeed. You are known to like to control things, especially the people you love. Just like the Chariot energy, you have a shell similar to the armor of the rider in this card. This shell is used to protect your sensitive, kind, and caring inner nature. Because you are easily hurt, it's important for you to listen to your intuition and gut instincts about people. Take control and trust your instincts.

Many people believe Cancer is prone to depressed moods and this can be true. Cancer's planetary ruler is the moon, which heightens the likelihood of ebbs and flows of feelings. Just like the crab with its hard shell, you will need to protect yourself in order to survive. Having boundaries is key and this card reminds you of the need to balance your emotions with practical responsibilities. There is a push and pull between being vulnerable and fighting for self-protection. Cancer, just like the Chariot archetype, likes taking horses by the reins, which symbolizes life. Controlling outcomes can bring a sense of peace, especially during times of crisis or change.

Sign Type: Water Element

Cancer is a water sign which makes you deeply emotional. Your sensitivity can make it difficult to be around others for too long. Withdrawing from the stress of the world and finding comfort with family and friends is beneficial. As a water sign, Cancer is known as one of the most intuitive signs of the zodiac. Your ability to feel complex emotions and ability to empathize with others is extraordinary. There is a depth to your personality and a hidden side to you that only those you trust will ever see. Because of your shell of protection, people might misjudge you and feel that you are cold or distant. This is how you fool people. You know how to protect yourself, mainly because you had to survive by learning at an early age to understand your feelings.

Personality Color: Blue

Cancer is a blue personality. You have the ability to nurture and help others in a calm and caring way. Blue personalities value emotions, relationships, and helping others. These are all the things you do best. As a blue, you need to learn to protect your energy. Having strong boundaries and listening to others' feelings comes naturally. Implementing grounding exercises and spending time in solitude can help you heal. At work you are the person who notices the small details in social situations. If someone is struggling or seems stressed you are a great listener. Ensuring other people are happy can be fulfilling. You are often found taking care of others and drawn to the helping professions. Relationships with others, especially your family, take center stage. You care more about how people are feeling than most people. You like to nurture others and help people with their problems. Feeling needed helps you feel connected and valued. You get along well with the other blue personalities — Scorpio and Pisces.

The Cancer Current Life Relationship Landscape

If you were born under the sign of Cancer, finding people you can trust is part of your journey. You appreciate friends and lovers who support your goals without judging you. Your emotions might sometimes seem complex to people, but you likely accept this as a natural part of you. Warming up to others may take some time before you let them really know you. You want your privacy to be respected but don't want those you love to stay away for too long.

The traditional astrology phrase for your sign is "I feel." However there are occasions you want to rest your emotions and recharge your mental energy. You don't mind people depending on you but value those who let you lean on them in return.

Intimacy with a special person in your life gives you a sense of security. Those who understand your need for a peaceful home life become true friends. Connecting intuitively with people is a spiritual or mystical experience. You could meet individuals in surprising ways as though it was a special synchronicity or a meaningful coincidence.

You have a caring side but probably don't want to reveal this too quickly. If you feel love for someone your nurturing tendencies come out as powerful as a sunrise. If your feelings get hurt you will spontaneously close off your inner world until you find it safe to come back out.

Your loyalty to others can last for a lifetime. Preserving a relationship you value is a heartfelt part of you. Building milestones with a lover through shared goals can become important to you. There are times your ideals will guide you to a unique plan for self-discovery. You need to do this as it empowers the bond you feel for others. You are attracted to people who act like they know how to express feelings.

The Cancer Past Life Karmic Relationship Patterns

Everyone has past life memories, whether conscious of them or not. You probably will not identify with each of the karmic relationship patterns that will be discussed. If one or more of them speak to you, don't let it worry you. Each of us came here to grow and learn how to overcome past life patterns. In recognizing a pattern, you will begin to perceive how to make peace with it. It does take time and practice to gain a new understanding of this energy.

As a Cancer your talent in processing experiences to see how they can fit into your life will help you in overcoming a past life pattern. It is not unusual to feel like you are right back where you started in dealing with one of these patterns. That is okay. If you keep moving forward, the hold of a pattern will diminish right before your eyes sooner than you think.

I Feel Invisible

This past life pattern can come to life for more than one reason. Sometimes it might feel like you have been taken for granted. It is as though you are expected to go along with the program of others. Your voice gets drowned out by the louder words of the people around you. You may be experiencing a pattern that has followed you into this incarnation if it sounds all too familiar. Your own dreams can be difficult to turn into reality. It may be true you are living out the hopes and wishes of someone else with your own kept behind the scenes. Your intuitive instincts get bottled up in this past life influence. It can be your over-sensitivity in not wanting to disappoint people that has you locked into this way of thinking.

Mood Swings

The water element that rules Cancer has the capacity to take you deep within yourself. Because the moon is your ruling planet, you are prone to extremes of emotions that can ebb and flow. The cycles of the moon can affect you greatly. You might benefit by paying attention to how you are feeling during a full moon for instance. There are occasions when someone might wonder what is on your mind. You may appear to be experiencing some type of mood suddenly. You probably think of this as a normal way to think things through. This pattern can be problematic if you are holding onto intense feelings without verbalizing a response to actions by others. You are likely to explode toward someone more than you might if you did not hide your feelings. Moods can get out of control if you can't get faster response time to situations that really need your honest input. Anger builds when you try to bury it and can bring out moody confrontations you want to avoid.

Dependency Needs Imbalance

If this past life pattern makes its presence felt, it takes the form of creating dependency issues. Every relationship requires an equal exchange of emotional support when needed. It is when you start to lose your own unique footing in a relationship that you can easily lose sight of your own goals. Sometimes this pattern occurs if you start leaning so heavily on someone that it throws the relationship off center, which translates to out of balance. If you expect someone to take on too much responsibility it can take away from your sense of personal power.

There is another way this pattern takes shape. It is when you enable others to lean on you too heavily. The burden of this weight takes its toll on your mental strength. You may become very emotionally drained. It is possible this past life pattern is coming at you through other people with dependency issues of their own. You are getting a chance here to see the pattern coming at you through others. If you enable the behavior to continue, it keeps you from the relationship harmony you would like to attain.

Walking On the Moon
Water signs like yourself have a strong emotional nature. You will occasionally find your intuitive expression well out in front of your mental articulation. If this pattern enters the scene, you could feel overwhelmed by the mental input from other individuals. Why does this happen? That powerful intuition you possess might sensitize you in a big way to the energy of people. The closer you get to someone in a relationship, the more you may feel like you can't hold on to your own identity. It may be that in some past lives this was a reality. Sometimes being involved with certain people can bring out this pattern as a repeat performance. It might feel familiar, like you keep replaying a scene or statement. You have a very active intuition that gets entangled with emotional confusion if you are in relationships that have an overwhelming impact on you.

Trouble Receiving

As a Cancer you are known to nurture and support those people you care about. You channel the universe as a giver of yourself to others. That is wonderful. However, if this pattern is too big a part of your everyday life in relationships, it denotes you are not as good at receiving for various reasons. One of the reasons might be that you don't feel you deserve to receive love from others.

It might be that you are too busy trying to make everybody else feel good about themselves. You may have closed down importing love and affection. You excel at exporting your emotional support to people but have grown uncomfortable in receiving. It could come down to not wanting to become vulnerable. An inability to let people give back to you could prevent you from gaining a more total experience of relationship fulfillment.

Homebody

A need for privacy is in the DNA of the sign Cancer. This past life pattern materializes when you retreat into solitude as an escape. Everyone needs downtime from a busy life; even space from our important people can be healthy. If it is more running away due to a fear of making a commitment to a relationship, then this pattern becomes a problem. It might be you have given up on finding closeness with someone due to not wanting to take the risk of being emotionally hurt. Staying in the confines of your own comfort zones can cause you to miss out on finding a compatible partner. It could be that memories in your consciousness from past lives have resurfaced from this pattern, causing a hesitation to trust relationships will bring the happiness you desire.

Digging Up the Seed

This past life pattern introduces itself to you in different ways. One is when you start out happy with a relationship but suddenly you want to slam on the brakes for no apparent reason. You begin to doubt that it could possibly be true that you have met the right person. It usually comes down to over-analyzing the relationship. You begin to look for flaws that may or may not be there in the other person. The root of this pattern can be a fear that in the end, the relationship will not succeed. Sometimes your emotional intensity crosses over into self-doubt that can cloud your perceptions. It might be that a failure to communicate your worries with a partner only serves to make this pattern a problem.

This pattern could come in the form of manifesting relationship partners that display this behavior. It may come down to their own lack of faith in themselves that they can sustain a long-term relationship. This sometimes occurs to give you an opportunity to see the pattern in someone else without you having to repeat this behavior yourself.

Territorial Tension

Being born as a Sun sign, comfort zones are important to a Cancer. Home, and to some degree having the privacy you prefer, are highly valued. This pattern can come along in a relationship if someone disturbs your favorite ways of living your everyday life. Your identity can feel confused if a person is trying to tell you how to live your life. Your good instincts, that know when people are invading your territorial rights, could be in a fog. Power struggles have a tendency to distance you from people. Your own goals and the way you want to approach them become a very personal need. Your need to claim some downtime from a relationship has to be honored for you to feel right and comfortable with a person. This could very well be a pattern lodged deep in your past life memory bank.

Past Fears

Becoming comfortable with a new partner is challenging if you can't get let go of memories of previous relationships in the current incarnation that did not go well. This becomes an even deeper pattern when memories of unfulfilling relationships from past lives get activated. Your sign, Cancer, has a well-developed memory which at times will serve you well. If there is emotional pain baked into that memory, it can distort your perceptions of a current, important person in your life. It might be a challenge to navigate around what has not made you happy previously in relationships, so you can settle into new ones. It might be you are projecting onto someone images still in your mind from previous encounters, from this lifetime or from past incarnations that disappointed you.

Too Much Insensitivity

You can be standing near someone, yet still feel a world apart, if this pattern is pulsating too strongly in your mind. You don't have to always be expressing feelings, but if you hold all of them back then intimacy is difficult to establish with someone. People could feel they have to pry out your emotions to get an idea of who you might be within yourself. If you are perceived as insensitive too often, it keeps people at a distance. This past life pattern may not be part of your conscious understanding. It usually lurks behind the scenes in subconscious past life memories. But when activated, it can make expressing emotions a real challenge. If you want to bring a lover or anyone closer, this pattern will need to be brought out into the open landscape to gain a new understanding of how it impacts you.

Too Caring

Your sign, Cancer, can attract people into your life who need a great deal of attention. This past life pattern can be traced back to previous lives where you took being overprotective too far. If you fall into this behavior in this lifetime, it can cause others to be too dependent on you. Being emotionally supportive of those you care about is a good thing. It is when you feel responsible too much of the time for someone that your relationship can get out of balance. You can become too drained of energy if you are carrying too much of the weight in relationships. You may like being counted on by your friends, family and lovers, but when you lose sight of your boundaries is when you get into trouble.

Feelings of Insecurity

Finding a sense of security is a heartfelt need you want to maintain. If a relationship starts to eat away at your inner stability it brings you great discomfort. Your intuition is probably sounding an alarm to remind you that this is a past life pattern you came into this life to avoid. Your affection or feelings of attachment to someone could cause you to deny the reality of how that person is causing you mental anxiety. Your intuition may be trying to guide you away from a person who is not giving you the love you badly want to receive. A refusal to see with clearer vision might keep you entangled in this pattern far longer than is good for you.

The Cancer Reward for Using Your Sixth Sense Intuitive Perception to Solve Relationship Karmic Patterns

You could experience a sigh of relief as you make your way through a karmic pattern's influence. This does often occur. It might even energize a current relationship with bold new insights. The confidence you gain in just recognizing the presence of a pattern allows you to walk along a more productive path. You could experience a feeling that the effort was well worth it, to turn a past life pattern into a sense of renewal. Relationships might seem easier to form and your ability to create greater harmony with others is possible.

Try to keep in mind if you feel a connection with a karmic pattern that you can gain a new perspective on this energy. It can seem difficult at first to get out from under the influence of a pattern if it has been with you in this life for a long time. Your steady determination to put into practice a new awareness is the key to opening the door to overcoming a pattern. Sometimes it is a retraining of our mind to not give in to the pull of a pattern's shadowy energy. The light is closer than you might think. Opening your eyes to a renewed reality starts an exciting process that will unfold into a wonderful self-discovery.

The I Feel Invisible pattern becomes a lighter background noise as you become more assertive. If at first this is a foreign experience to act in this way, don't let it bother you. Before you know it, people will treat you with more recognition. Giving yourself permission to be self-oriented is a bold first step in pushing this past life pattern out of the current life. Since you are one of the water signs by being a Cancer, your intuition might instinctively put a quiet space into your thought processes. This is fine as sometimes the tranquility is your own way of sizing up situations. There is a need, though, to step out from the serenity and take action. You will find your own goals and ideas getting support when you don't tolerate those people negating your important plans. In putting yourself first, the universe will guide you to relationships that promise fulfillment.

The Mood Swings pattern is more likely to be less problematic when you verbalize your feelings. Moods in themselves are not a bad thing. Sometimes they can launch you into a new way of thinking. They can act as a barometer on how you are feeling about interactions with others. If held back, and emotions are allowed to build into angry moods, then this pattern intensifies. It is far better to communicate with people you want to bring closer. Intimacy is easier to have with those you love when bringing your most heartfelt feelings further out into the open. When you reveal what is on your mind, trust and even passion become a reality with the important people in your life.

The Dependency Needs Imbalance may sneak up on you when you least expect it. But with practice and consistent effort you can turn this past life pattern into less of a problem rather quickly. Your own self-reliance balanced with knowing you can count on a trusted partner keeps this pattern in check. In every relationship there will be times when a person can be going through a difficult time period and needs help from a lover or friend. To keep this pattern from repeatedly entering your life, focusing on your own goals may be one way to break free. Tuning into your own independence will empower you.

If you are in a relationship with a person expecting you to do the impossible for them on a regular basis, you will get emotionally drained. It is better for you to back off from trying to do too much. You will need to communicate what you can and cannot continually do for someone. Clearly defining your boundaries is the way to transcend this pattern.

The Walking on the Moon pattern may require you to find techniques that keep you grounded in relating to others. Your own energy is well equipped to stay mentally and emotionally clear to avoid a spaced-out feeling. It might be good to explore meditation or yoga as a way to strengthen your inner connection to your more sensitive energy. Intuition can be a road to empowerment as you let it get expressed. There are certain individuals who, because of the chemistry they form with you, can cause you to feel off center. There may be occasions when you will need to pull back to gather your own energies. Believing in the inner power you possess goes a long way to giving you the confidence to rise above this past life influence.

The Trouble Receiving pattern is best resolved by allowing yourself to receive emotional support as well as giving it to others. You need to replenish your own energy by receiving. If you are constantly giving, you can feel drained of physical, mental and emotional energy. There is a healing quality in receiving. It can give strength to your intuition as well by taking in what others are trying to give back to you. The universe wants you to balance giving and receiving. It is in this sharing that you step out of this pattern and enjoy greater relationship fulfillment.

The Hermit pattern is part of the natural inclination to want privacy as a member of the Cancer family. It indicates that there is a need at times to seek out time alone even if you have discovered a soul mate. The key thing is to communicate to others that you find it centering to be in your own space. You probably find it easier to process the past and present when getting private time alone. If you take the risk of including others in your ideas it brings them closer. This pattern does have a way of weaving a wall of seclusion around you if you fear letting others into your life. If you find the courage to take small steps to venture out, you allow the universe to bring the people you need for happiness into your life. If you have faith in your intuition, it will guide you to form relationships with individuals who respect your need for privacy and enjoy the time shared together.

The Digging up the Seed pattern can indicate that the way out of this past life pattern is to stick around in a relationship at the first signs of adversity. Sometimes it is in facing the problems that the deeper harmony breaks through. It takes time for a relationship to truly reveal itself. If you can focus more on the positives in being with a person than the negatives, then it often opens the door to clearer communication. Don't feel bad if you prefer short-term relationships. But if you are desiring a long-term commitment, believing you have much to offer could be the key to making this happen. Accepting the fact there are no perfect people takes some of the intensity out of this pattern. Patience is an important part of gaining clarity and finding the relationship fulfillment you wish to attain.

If it is more that this pattern appears in the form of other people in your life, it gives you an opportunity to perceive this. If you are wanting to stay in relationships with those who have adopted this pattern it can be disappointing. The main thing is that you are not denying what you see. You will be closer to finding the right person for you when identifying this pattern manifesting through someone else. It is the universe showing you that this is a pattern you don't want to accept.

When you make your goals and priorities clear to others there is less of a chance the Territorial Tension pattern will prevail. At least you will have staked your claim to your own turf in a relationship. Your own empowerment and passion come forward faster when you assertively walk your walk. To keep this pattern from repeating in this incarnation you may need to make some compromises. Your intuition finds strength when you feel inner stability. Your relationships benefit greatly when you know your own personal power is respected. A feeling of independence keeps this pattern away from you and points the way to creating relationship harmony.

The Past Fears pattern takes some practice in not superimposing experiences from the past onto new relationship encounters. This pattern can suddenly emerge in a current relationship that has been going on for a while. It helps to begin to realize that negative memories have no power over you. You need to replace them with as many positive images in your mind as possible. It does take some work to release a past or current life memory, to keep it from interfering with the happiness you want to have in your life. If you find success in one wholesome relationship it can heal all of those past memories. You might be surprised at how fast this process can take place.

To keep the Too Much Insensitivity pattern out of your relationships, all you need to do is make a more conscious effort to express feelings. The water element that colors the sign Cancer can influence you to be cautious about sharing your inner world. In showing you care about someone through your words and actions is a bold first step beyond the border of this pattern. If, for whatever reason, you are not comfortable with the emotional side of life, you don't need to always say how you feel. If you are a good listener it proves to others you are really there for them. If you take the risk occasionally to speak about what you are feeling, it opens the door to greater intimacy, passion and the fulfillment you long to have.

The Too Caring pattern only becomes a reality if you try to do too much for others. There is a natural drive in being a Cancer to be very loyal to those you care about. Reaching out to support those people you are close to is important to you. There are times, when you allow a partner to find their own footing in dealing with a problem, that it empowers them. It is a delicate balance to know when to take a hands-on or hands-off approach in letting someone take responsibility for a decision. With practice you can get good at doing this. Your emotional and mental energy stays clearer and stronger to help people when you keep a clear sense of boundaries.

The Feelings of Insecurity pattern need not interfere with your relationship happiness. A Sun sign person like yourself is like a fish out of water when not feeling internally stable in relationships. Your sense of identity and creative passion in your soul needs to know people respect your need for emotional peace. You aren't afraid to go through adversity with a partner. Each time the two of you face problems together it secures your trust for each other. You keep this past life pattern from interfering with your relationship fulfillment by letting your intuition guide you to individuals valuing peace of mind as much as you do.

The Cancer Reward from Solving Karmic Patterns

When you first realize a karmic pattern has followed you into this life it is an opportunity to overcome the influence. Don't judge yourself as having done something wrong but rather celebrate in gaining new insight. Your Cancer intuition and mental power has found a new ally in tuning into the confidence to put a pattern to rest. It is a journey when you take those first steps in rising above a past life pattern. You will sense a renewed energy in getting a broader perspective about past life energies. What was once a shadowy force, possibly causing self-doubt, becomes a beacon of light, shining rays of a new bold confidence upon you.

It does take putting new understanding into practice to keep a pattern at a distance. You could be surprised at how fast you can integrate your comprehension of past life energies in a positive way into the current incarnation. Don't get discouraged if you take a step back in trying to walk past the hold of a pattern. Keep a positive attitude and you will achieve the growth you desire.

Stay patient and the path forward is easier to attain. Inner clarity and relationship harmony are wonderful rewards in transcending past life patterns. Fulfilling relationship experiences will greet you when you gain new perceptions to face the challenge represented by a past life pattern.

Cancer the Caregiver Journal Prompts

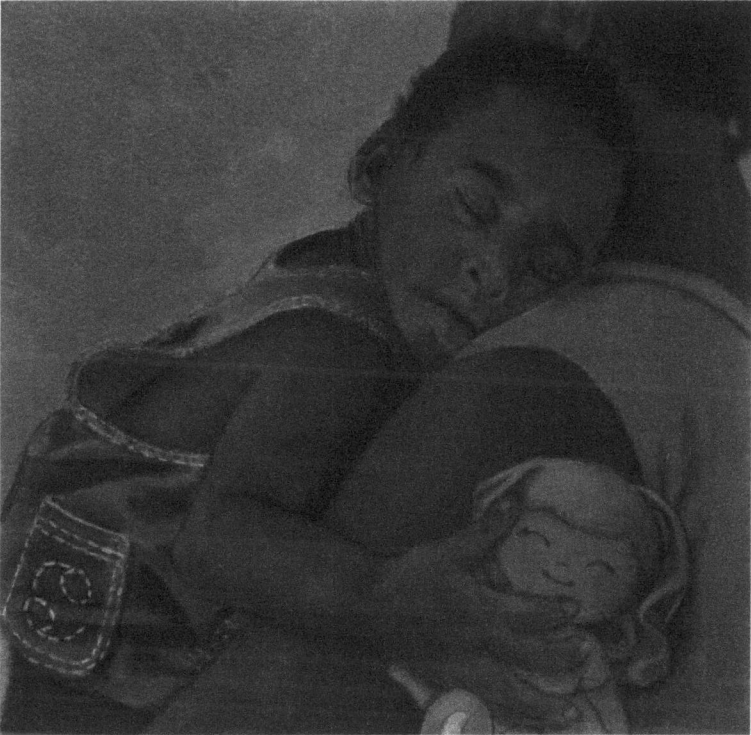

1. How do you feel when you see the Cancer image?
2. What Cancer archetype traits do you resonate with?
3. How do you nurture and take care of others?
4. How do you nurture yourself?
5. Is your home and family important to you?
6. How do you tap into your intuition?
7. What past life patterns have you experienced?

Chapter Five

Leo the Creator or Artist

"I WILL"

Keywords: Creative, Courageous, Willful, Brave, Confident, Outgoing

Sun Sign Dates: July 22–August 21

Temperament: Choleric

Sign Type: Fire, Fixed

Planetary Ruler: Sun

Jungian Archetype: Creator or Artist

Tarot Card: Strength

Polar Opposite Archetype: The Outlaw or Rebel

Astrology Nickname: The Leader

Polar Opposite Sign: Aquarius

Symbol: The Lion

Personality Color: Gold, Extroverted

Rules: The Fifth House; Heart, Circulatory System

Temperament: Choleric

Leo is the fifth sign of the zodiac. You are passionate, energetic, and vibrant. Just like the choleric temperament, you are filled with ambition and courage. Assertive, confident, and charming you energize the room. People notice you immediately because of your bright light. As a natural leader, you have a charismatic personality and a light that shines brightly, attracting many friends. Your enthusiasm inspires others, and they like to follow you. You are filled with ambition, energy, and enthusiasm. Assertive and self-assured you are able to energize and motivate others to change. As a natural leader, you have an artistic and creative side. Your personality shines brightly and you easily attract many friends and associates. There is a flirtatious and fun-loving side to your personality which makes people love being around your positive energy. As a choleric personality, you are determined and pursue your desires fiercely. You can be hot tempered and prideful when things don't go your way. As a Leo, you are strong willed and can get irritable if you don't feel loved. It's important for you to feel appreciated and respected in order to be happy.

Jungian Archetype: Artist or Creator

Leo is known as the entertainer of the zodiac. You are born with natural artistic abilities and have a very creative side to your personality. Self-expression is important for you to feel happy. As the artist and creator archetype, you like to be noticed and recognized for your unique gifts. Whether your gift is sports, music, painting, or acting, being in the limelight can be fulfilling. As an artist, you need time to pursue your special hobbies. You are imaginative and get bored easily with routine. Creating new ways to work or do things can fulfill your deep desire for creating inspiration. Leos have a need to feel love and to show love. You are one of the most romantic signs and enjoy creating poetry, love songs, and buying gifts for the people you love. Feeling passionate emotions can ignite your creative juices.

Tarot Card Archetype: Strength

The lion symbol in the Strength card symbolizes generosity, royalty, and courage. In astrology, you are known to also be strong, courageous, and affectionate. Your symbol is the Lion, just like in this card, and it embodies intense strength. In this card you will see the lion revealing its vulnerability and also its desire to overcome life's challenges. The female in the center of the card taming the lion is wearing flowers in her hair, which represents innocence. This can also be connected to Leo's famous mane of thick hair. The infinity symbol above her head relates to the endless supply of energy and natural strength you possess as a Leo. You are driven to succeed and often have good luck with your endeavors at a young age. Doors seem to open easily for you.

Sign Element: Fire

As a Leo, your personality is strong and burns bright, just like the fire element. Your energy is warm to the touch, just like the sun beaming down, and makes others feel loved instantly. As a fire sign, you're dynamic and have a big-hearted approach to showing affection. Passionate, you need romance in your life. You want to take charge of situations and can naturally lead others. People follow you and listen to your advice. It's good because you don't like to be told what to do. You have a confidence and boldness that others respect. Your charismatic approach and outgoing ways attract many allies into your life. Having fun and experiencing pleasure are important to you. Bringing joy into other people's lives comes easily and you have an ability to highlight other people's strengths. But you want attention and sometimes find it hard not to have recognition. You like to feel special, be valued, and respected. You are good at making others feel special too. You have a strong desire to express yourself freely and fiercely, just like the fire element.

Personality Color: Orange

Leo is associated with the orange personality temperament. You are positive, impulsive, charming, and friendly. You like a challenge and taking risks. As an orange, you can inspire others and can support them in achieving their goals. Working with groups of people is where you shine and you are often found out front or center stage. When you speak, people listen, and you have a natural ability to share your creative ideas. Motivating others is your forte and people enjoy being around you. Your outgoing and confident nature makes you magnetic and attractive. Change is important to you and pursuing new experiences. You can grow bored and restless at times, and like excitement and the thrill of life. Orange personalities are affectionate and need physical touch more than most people. Your nature is loving and you want to feel needed and cherished. Romantic relationships are important to your well-being. If you have love in your life, then you can be fiercely loyal and protective of others.

The Leo Current Life Relationship Landscape

If you were born under the sign of Leo, you want the world to take notice of you. Your personality, when confident, often opens up new adventures in meeting people. You enjoy individuals knowing how to celebrate life. Those who aren't afraid to share their goals and ideas openly attract your attention. There are times when you are quieter, particularly when it comes to letting others know your most heartfelt dreams. People who like to laugh and yet have serious plans pique your interest. The traditional slogan in astrology for your sign is "I create." People who naturally have a creative drive stimulate your mind.

There is an underlying sensitivity that might be revealed to someone you spend a lot of time with. You are at your best when inspiring others to act with confidence. You can be a cheerleader who wins the hearts of your closest companions. It is that look in your eyes that says you really care about a person that keeps them close.

If you pay attention to the needs of someone it ignites the passion and intimacy in being together. Independent individuals intrigue you. You are at your best when encouraging others to explore their own goals but don't necessarily want them to wander too far ahead without you.

People who support your own goals win your loyalty. Your pride, to remain strong, sometimes needs strokes of attention.

You can be a loner but soon miss the touch and feel of a loved one. When you show your love and affection with no motives, the universe rewards you with abundance and the love you need.

The Leo Past Life Karmic Relationship Patterns

Past life memories have followed everyone into this lifetime. Each of us has certain past patterns that can get activated in the current incarnation. If one or more of the patterns being discussed seems familiar, don't let it bother you. Just think of it as leftover homework from previous lives needing to be completed. Go at your own pace. This is not a competition nor a racing event. In dealing with a pattern, you are embarking on a journey of self-discovery. Think of it as the universe trying to get you to alter a behavior to allow more fulfilling experiences to unfold.

As a Leo, your ability to state an intended goal and reach it is always within your grasp. Karmic patterns need not stand in the way of finding harmony with special people. Don't worry if you seem to be repeating a behavior. With that lion-like roar from the depth of your sign, there is no past life influence that cannot be resolved. It will make your steps lighter and your path to relationship happiness easier to attain when you begin to tune into past life patterns. With regular effort it will be possible to channel the energy of a past pattern into creative directions.

Center Stage Is Always Mine

The sign Leo has a natural impulse to attract attention. If this urge gets out of control it brings this pattern into your life. Sharing the stage in your everyday life makes others feel valued. If someone begins to get the feeling their own goals are getting too dominated by your own aspirations, resentment can become a reality. If this past life pattern is too big a part of your everyday life, people lose trust that you will support their own most important goals. Sometimes a pattern like this one is not in the awareness of the conscious mind. It is hidden in our subconscious and interferes with the harmony we would like to have with others.

Another way this pattern appears is if you are attracting individuals into your life sporting this behavior. The universe could be offering you an opportunity to observe the behavior in others to allow you to realize that this is a past life pattern you want to avoid. In other words, it is your own potential pattern but before embracing it you can gain the insight to choose not to enter into it.

Lack of Ego Strength

Leo is known to be a strong lion. In some past lives that inner fortitude lost its way and was too diluted. Your self-confidence became too negated from the input of others. This past life pattern might be getting in the way of your creative thinking. Your movement forward to pursue meaningful relationships can become impacted as well. You may not feel deserving of a wonderful soul mate. This is a pattern that can find you backing off from forming a commitment with someone that could be the right person for you. You could be blocking the positive support people are trying to offer you. A Leo like you feels like something is badly missing without a natural heartbeat of self-assurance.

Too Much Pride

A fear of failure can be the root cause of this pattern. Being proud of yourself is a good thing as it often ignites inspiring goals. This past life pattern, if activated, can get you to think a relationship will not succeed due to self-doubt. If you hide this way of thinking, it will cause confusion within your own mind and in that of others. People will become alienated if you sit on fear of failure for long periods. This pattern will at times make it difficult for you to let others tune into your emotional nature.

You will be perceived as having a wall around you, making it hard for others to enter. True communication becomes a tall order to attain. Often at the root of this past life pattern is a negative outlook that may be blocking the fulfillment you can have. A refusal to talk about the issues you are hiding results in a great distance between you and others. A fear of showing any vulnerability is another indication that this past life influence has made an appearance.

Compulsive Need for Love

If this pattern followed you into this incarnation, it is a driving force to keep confirming you need love. The problem with this is when you are never satisfied with any relationship. It can be caused by more than one reason. One is a low self-esteem. In this instance it doesn't matter who you are with in this pattern, you do not feel deserving of the relationship. It does not mean in all of your past lives this was a problem, it is only in those lives where this type of thinking grew too strong. It kept you then, and possibly now, moving impulsively from one relationship to another without much clear thinking. Another offshoot of this past life influence was searching for that perfect person. It became an endless frustration to satisfy an impossible quest. You were never really happy in that you could not accept others the way they were. Your life too often lacked stability. If this pattern visits you too often in your current life, then a feeling of discontent is often a reality.

Moving Too Impulsively Fast

You are a Leo fire sign that can get moving spontaneously in the fast lane. If you find yourself too impatient with people, then there is a good possibility that this tendency is a past life carryover. This could appear to others as if you are too easily distracted from paying attention to them. People will feel you are not present even while in the same room. Listening and real communication is not as vibrant as it needs to be. Closeness and intimacy become too absent with those you want to keep near you. Your own life goals begin to drown out those of lovers and friends. Not making time for important people causes them to drift away. Losing sight of supporting the goals of others weakens their trust if this pattern is a regular visitor.

Too Tight-Lipped

Leo is known as being dramatic and at times outspoken. If you are very quiet when your feelings are hurt and have a tendency to hide your emotions, it could be linked to this past life pattern. There are times you may want to process your thoughts before reacting to situations. It is if you are in the habit of not stating directly your ideas that it can confuse others. This occurs for different reasons. One may be that in some past lives your opinions were discounted and even ignored. It could be that in your memory resides this painful recollection; it is causing you to fall back into this behavior. Another possibility for this past life pattern to manifest is due to not trusting someone. You go on the defensive by not revealing how you really feel when asked for some input of your own ideas. If you stay attached to this pattern your closeness with others becomes turned into distance.

Hurt Ego

Your persona that you show the world may be a mask to conceal a very sensitive side of you. Criticism may be something that sends your mind into a tailspin. This is a past life pattern that can find you overreacting to circumstances that might surprise people you are close to. You might wonder why very suddenly you allow some people to rub you up the wrong way. This pattern can bring out angry outbursts that can give you a sense of losing control. You are a card-carrying Leo which means you have natural instincts to maintain a solid, stabilizing life. This pattern reveals an inner world that you came into this life to heal. It shows that in some past lives perhaps you took in more criticism than you could handle. Certain people or situations will act as a trigger, igniting this pattern and sometimes causing you to act in ways you later wish had not occurred.

Ignoring Your Limits

A fire sign like yourself as a Leo might be tempted to take unnecessary risks. This is a past life pattern that could boldly find you entering relationships not in your best interest. You could be partnering with people more focused on their own goals and ignoring your own. The equality you are hoping for is tilted too far toward others. This begins to take away from your happiness in a big way. You may have been attracted to someone at first sight that looked like the right match for you. If you deny the reality that your needs are not being met, you may stay in these types of relationships far too long. That Leo courage to explore the unknown and seek new adventure needs to be directed to a relationship that promises greater fulfillment. The problem this past life pattern can present is that it plays on your drive to maintain a relationship, even if it is not what it had promised to be.

Fixed Opinions

You have great persistence to follow through on plans you want to achieve. If this past life pattern finds its way into your life, a tendency to hold onto your own viewpoints may clash with others. When flexibility is missing too frequently people can react with anger. You can appear like an immovable force. Those you love will start to distance themselves if you continue to act in this way. Sometimes this pattern appears when you feel a need to stay in control of the outcome of decisions with people. It is what looks like your lack of openness to alternative ideas that can cause tension in communicating with others. If you fail to listen to opposing views or suggestions as a regular occurrence, it does not get the cooperation you want. Compromise is too much of a foreign word in your mind.

Bullying

Promoting your ideas comes naturally for you as a Leo, it is when you are forcing your plans on others to get your own way that this past life pattern intensifies. It doesn't mean in past incarnations you always demonstrated this behavior. It could even be this memory is linked to particular lives where you were too overpowered by others, and it is triggering an overreactive use of this tendency. If you get too pushy it will cause others to react angrily. The main effect of this pattern is that it keeps the harmony and greater love you hope to achieve with someone from happening. Realizing you can get more of what you need through trusting your closest companions is missing. Exhibiting a bullying behavior keeps the closeness with others at a distance.

Trying Too Hard to Impress

This pattern implies that in some past lives you went out of your way to impress others as a way to be liked. If the pattern finds you riding into extremes, it takes away from forming genuine connections with others. There is nothing wrong with wanting to be perceived favorably. It is if you are giving an exaggerated portrayal of yourself that it can cause confusion when wanting to establish an intimate relationship. Everyone has an outward personality they show the world. This pattern, if becoming too regularly used, gets in between you and those you are trying to bring close. It presents a challenge to others to break through what feels and looks like a wall around you.

Angry Moods

Letting anger build is a path backtracking into this past life pattern. It is when holding back your feelings that the anger starts to become war clouds. You may be launching into angry outbursts over circumstances totally unrelated to how the anger started in the first place. Rather than being in the moment with how you feel, this pattern entices you into holding back your emotional intensity. Sooner or later that squashed-down anger comes firing out. You are a fire sign that does better when you are open about your ideas and insights. There is a good chance those who know you the best will sense there is something bothering you. When your timing is off in expressing anger, it creates disruption and tension in your relationships.

The Leo Reward for Using Your Sixth Sense Intuitive Perception to Solve Karmic Relationship Patterns

You will feel like you have more energy and a brighter outlook on life when releasing a karmic pattern from your mind. The world seems full of opportunities when letting go of a past life shadowy energy. The balance and harmony in relationships seem to magically be easier to attain. Attracting compatible partners has an easier flow. Your insights into what you need in a relationship might become clearer.

If any of the karmic patterns discussed hit a nerve in you, don't let it bother you. The important thing is identifying if a pattern of behavior is interfering with your ability to enjoy fulfillment in how you relate to others. This is the first step to gaining the clarity to turn the energy into a more productive expression. You may be surprised by your own ability to transcend a past life pattern by just becoming more aware of the tendency to repeat a pattern. A new path of self-discovery unfolds when you gain a new perception and attitude in learning how to let go of a pattern. Your mental, physical and intuitive energy gains strength when no longer allowing a past life pattern to be a reality.

When you share the power in a relationship the Center Stage Is Always Mine pattern will disappear as though it was never there. In empowering others, you bring a sense of wholesome equality into your relationships. People will know you value them, and you will be developing a great mutual support system. If this is a very ingrained pattern it won't change overnight, but with some consistent practice you will begin to recognize earlier if you are stepping too far into someone else's space. Your sign Leo needs a great deal of personal freedom. That elbow room you require is needed by your friends, family members and lovers as well.

If you are inviting people into your life that don't respect your own territory, think of it as an opportunity to recognize this as perhaps a past life pattern that was once a big part of you. This is your chance to realize that you don't need to go back into playing out this role again. You will likely find that someone lost in this pattern is not the right person to keep in your everyday life.

If the Lack of Ego Strength pattern is shadowing you in this incarnation it symbolizes you are needing to embody a bolder expression of yourself. The good news is that when manifesting the colors of the fiery sign Leo, you can tune into the assertiveness you require. When you walk and talk with confidence, it strengthens your identity, and you are more likely to land in relationships that bring harmony. It keeps away people that drown out your own self-expression when you project a belief in yourself. You were born under a sign that wants you to make your presence very visible. This is the roadmap to bring your relationships to rise to the level of fulfillment you prefer.

The Too Much Pride pattern can be channeled into a new direction by a willingness to let down your guard. You have more inner strength than you may realize at times. Your sign Leo sometimes gets empowered when responding to a challenge. The competitive power in you only needs to get focused in a new direction to turn the negative energy in this pattern into a winning formula for yourself. Letting others know when you are having trouble communicating, especially when you feel emotionally bottled up, can open the door to a deeper intimacy. Nobody expects you to always be a tower of strength. You find a sense of renewal by surrendering your fear of becoming vulnerable. What might have appeared to your mind as a weakness becomes a new source of strength in expressing honest communication.

The Compulsive Need for Love pattern can be overcome by coming to the realization that you deserve a fulfilling relationship. Developing a positive mindset goes far in keeping this past life pattern away from you. This pattern requires your patience as it might take some time to move in a new direction. You may not find a perfect partner, but you can be successful in being with a compatible person. The key thing to remember is that maintaining a new perspective in what will bring harmonious relationships into your life is important. In some ways this takes retraining your mind to find people who appreciate your ideas and who want an equal partnership. The compulsiveness to run to new relationships lessens as you grow comfortable with wanting stability.

The Moving Too Impulsively Fast pattern is not that difficult to convert into a more productive winning expression. It is amazing that when you show you are listening to the important people in your life, it makes love and friendship more vibrant. It is okay as a Leo to passionately pursue your own goals. If you slow down long enough to include others in big decisions it makes them feel valued. You are a fire sign so moving quickly comes naturally. Just remember not to lose sight of those you care about along your life journey. Clear communication gives a greater depth to your relationships and attracts the support you will always appreciate.

The Too Tight-Lipped pattern probably sounds counterintuitive for the sign Leo. Your sign will often push you to be direct. The closer you are to someone in your life, a past life tendency might intervene finding you holding back feelings. When you take the risk of revealing your emotional side, there is a greater chance to have the intimacy you desire. Sometimes it is that first leap of faith to boldly let your ideas be known that causes this pattern to recede. You may be surprised that with some practice in communicating more openly, this becomes a regular occurrence, and this pattern might seem like it never existed. Letting those you want to keep close into your inner world makes the relationships stronger. When you trust that it is okay to speak your heartfelt thoughts, it takes you on a path to greater harmony in how you relate to others.

The Hurt Ego pattern, if activated as a past life pattern, could be bringing up painful memories where you endured great opposition to your dreams. Leo is known for shaking off criticism and passionately pursuing life goals with a fiery spirit. There is a talent in compartmentalizing a problem to keep it from interfering with your life. If you can come to the realization that current relationship encounters may be bringing back past life memories, you will begin to overcome this pattern. This might be the source of tracing back your overreaction to people challenging your ideas. Learning to take a cool-down period to gain greater objectivity may help you gain the insight to get clarity about this past life pattern. It could take some time to transcend emotional bruises from past incarnations. Your patience in facing this pattern will pay great dividends along your life journey.

If you are in a relationship with someone overly critical in unreasonable ways, this pattern will likely keep resurfacing. It will require you to steer clear of people negating your every move in order for you to let go of this pattern. You don't need to search for perfect people. The main point here is discerning which individuals are wanting to take a similar path to harmony as yourself.

The Ignoring Your Limits pattern only needs you to take a reality check to make sure you did not rush into a relationship that looked promising but is not really in your best interest. If you stop denying that this is what you bargained for, you will be freer to move on to a more fulfilling relationship. It might take courage to move past someone not supporting your hopes and dreams. The Leo strength you possess could, at times, find you with overconfidence that you can change the person you are involved with in a relationship into something they are not willing to be. When you come to the realization that you have given the person every chance to change their behavior, with no results, the path to finding better options begins with this new awakened perception. Moving forward will feel like a refreshing breath of air to create relationships that give you as much as you are giving to someone else.

The Fixed Opinions pattern is not so hard to budge out of your way. If you show some degree of flexibility, it goes far in taking away the likelihood that this pattern will come between you and someone else. As a Leo, you can display that rugged determination to make your goals come true. There will be times your plans will conflict with the people closest to you. If you adopt a win-win strategy it brings others to support your needs because you are showing you want to do the same for them. You don't need to sacrifice your own dreams to please anyone. If you show you are not opposed to change and can adapt to new situations, your relationships do flow better. You actually get empowered through sharing your power.

The Bullying pattern is masking feelings of insecurity. Releasing a need to overpower others opens the door to new rewarding relationships. People will want to come closer. Trusting that you don't need to force your ideas on others is the first step out of this past life shadow. Your own goals will get the support you need when you realize that there is no need to manipulate people into your way of thinking. Through learning to trust your closest companions it makes falling into this pattern less likely. In walking away from a tendency to use this type of behavior, the fulfilling relationships you need are more likely to happen. In releasing the hold of this pattern, the universe responds by offering you alternative perceptions to attract the harmony in others you long to find.

The Trying Too Hard to Impress pattern need not remain a part of how you relate to individuals. When you reveal more of your natural thinking, people lock on to a faster clarity about you. This could be linked to certain past incarnations where you were not readily accepted for just being you. Coming out of the shadow of this pattern's influence only needs you to have more faith in yourself. It might not happen in one day but the more you practice not pretending to be someone you are not, the closer you are to finding fulfilling relationships. Small steps in a new direction will lead to eventually taking bigger ones. If you find the right people to have in your life, you don't need to act out a role that is not you. Revealing your authentic self wins the trust of individuals you want in your life.

The Angry Moods pattern need not be feared. Anger is an emotion that will leak out no matter how much any of us try to hide it. You are better off letting off some steam rather than letting hidden, intense feelings snowball out of control. There are times anger clears the air in relationships. If it is not used to manipulate or coerce you will find this pattern not so prevalent in your life. Forgiveness is a great ally if anger comes between you and someone else. Holding long grudges only serves to distance you from people. Learning to communicate your thoughts when feeling heated up over a situation might keep a problem from escalating. There are instances when a cooling-down period is wise, as long as you do come back and try to work out the issue with someone. The key thing to remember is waiting too long and sitting on anger has a tendency to make your perceptions unclear. There is much truth in dealing with a problem sooner rather than later to keep the peace with those you love.

The Leo Reward from Solving Karmic Patterns

Your Leo persistence to respond to the challenge of a karmic pattern paves the way for new insights. Once you have new eyes to see through a past life pattern, there is a great chance you will stay vigilant in not repeating the pattern. The Leo passion that colors your fiery spirit will rejoice in channeling a shadowy energy in positive directions. The personal empowerment in your footsteps will make your relationships ring with greater harmony.

Don't let it worry you if one or more of the past life patterns discussed has been a considerable part of your life journey. It is in gaining new insight into a past life pattern that provides bold new perceptions, giving you more opportunities to enjoy all of your relationships.

If you accept a need to be more flexible and accept change it makes it easier to overcome past life patterns. They have no real power over you. In stepping out of their influence through a new attitude of self-discovery, you could be surprised how the universe makes it possible to discover the joy you want to experience with the people you already know and the ones you are yet to meet.

Leo the Creator or Artist Journal Prompts

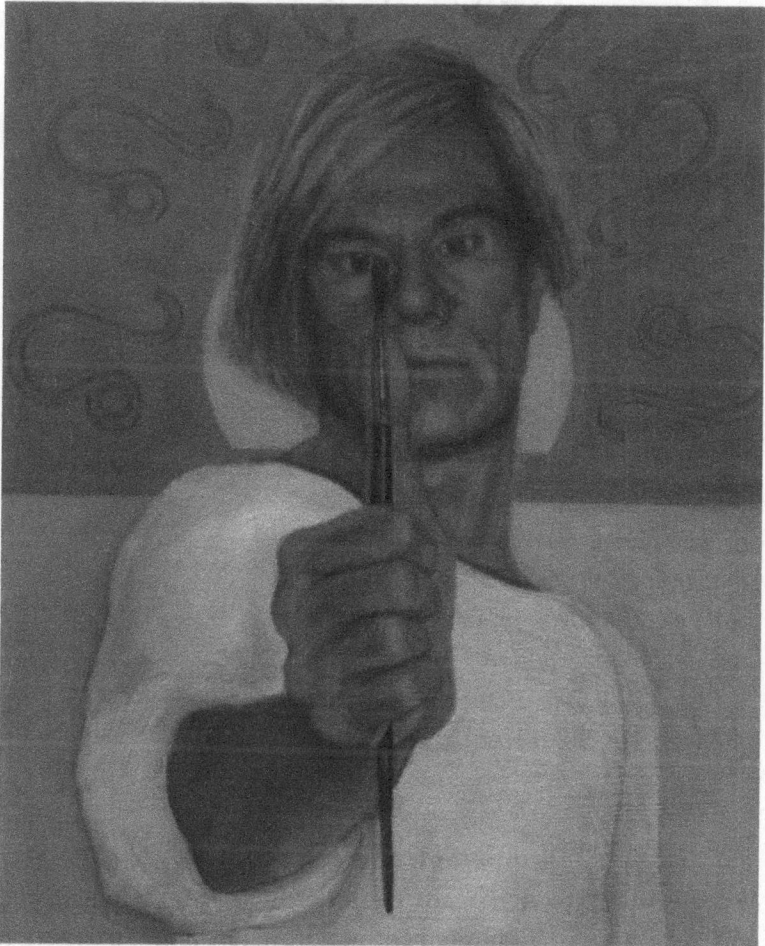

1. How do you feel when you see the Leo image?
2. What Leo archetype traits do you resonate most with?
3. Do you have artistic or creative talents?
4. What do you do for fun?
5. Do you enjoy children or want to have your own?
6. What leadership skills do you possess?
7. What past life patterns have you experienced?

Chapter Six

Virgo the Sage

"I ANALYZE"

Keywords: Intelligent, Detail-Oriented, Analytical, Servant, Modest, Efficient

Sun Sign Dates: August 22–September 21

Temperament: Melancholic

Sign Type: Earth, Mutable

Planetary Ruler: Mercury

Jungian Archetype: The Sage

Tarot Card: The Hermit

Polar Opposite Archetype: The Innocent

Astrology Nickname: The Perfectionist

Polar Opposite Sign: Pisces

Symbol: The Maiden

Personality Color: Gold, introverted

Rules: The Sixth House, The Stomach

Temperament: Melancholic

Virgo is the sixth sign of the zodiac. You are grounded, stable, and detail-focused. Implementing precision and analyzation are where you shine. You like to make things better and enjoy perfecting the world around you. Your perfectionism can sometimes lead to irritability and loneliness if you don't learn to balance your extremely hardworking nature. Virgo is associated with the melancholic temperament. As an earth sign, you are introverted and introspective. Efficiency and productivity make you feel good.

Similar to the melancholic personality, you are intellectual, thoughtful, modest, and super responsible. You are a deep thinker and enjoy communicating with others. Virgo is an adaptable sign and needs a solid routine in order to stay balanced. It's important for you to get enough sleep, eat healthily, and focus on balancing self-care.

Jungian Archetype: The Sage

Virgo is known as the maiden or the virgin. The symbol of purity resonates with your energy. Being a good person and helping others in need can be fulfilling. Sometimes you get a bad reputation for being too critical, but the truth is that you simply care too much. You want to make things better in the world. You want to help others and are a natural therapist because of your good communication skills. Taking care of others or working in a healthcare field is also attractive.

As the Sage archetype, you are wise, serious, and dutiful. Just like the Sage, Virgo wants to learn new things. But you want to collect knowledge that is meaningful in order to apply what you know in a practical way. Your goal is to help others improve their lives by giving guidance and bringing order to the world. Self-improvement and focusing on being healthy and having routines are important things to you. The Sage understands the importance of service and Virgos are modest, shy, and reserved. Like the Sage, you are an observer of the environment and are a down-to-earth and grounded soul.

You are a seeker of truth and soothing counselor, teacher, and healer. Helping others with getting organized, problem solving, and being supportive makes you feel useful.

Tarot Card Archetype: Hermit

Virgo is very similar to the Hermit personality card. The Hermit card represents wisdom, introspection, and solitude. As a Virgo, you need your alone time to decompress and slow down your active mind. You tend to analyze things and can obsess on your thoughts. Being alone helps you reflect and figure out your problems to find solutions.

Virgo energy is similar to the Hermit — it's soft spoken, pure, modest, and observant. You seek answers to problems and like to solve other people's problems. You are a genuine counselor and excellent advisor. Virgos believe in doing what is right and have a strong moral code. Speaking the truth and loyalty are important to you. Just like the Hermit, as a Virgo you grow stronger through experience and develop wisdom as you age.

You're a soul who is always on a quest for knowledge, perfection and wants to guide others toward self-improvement. In the Hermit card you can see the wizard holding the lantern. This symbolism is showing Virgo that they can find the answers to their problems by going within and listening to their intuition. Most answers in life can't be found through intellect and overanalyzing things. Sometimes you just have to be still and listen. Trusting your emotions will help you find answers.

Element: Earth

Virgo is an earth sign and known for being super reliable. As a practical soul, you like to feel in control of your world. Being an earth sign intensifies your desire to work hard and be productive. You are a high energy person and dedicated worker. There are very few people who can keep up with your level of efficiency. Your ability to multitask sets a high bar that most people can't achieve. Sometimes you have trouble relaxing and are prone to overthinking. It is important to make time to ground your energy, perhaps with practical mindfulness exercises, meditation, yoga, and learning to relax.

Helping others with practical duties makes you feel useful. You can also enjoy teaching and sharing your knowledge with others to help them be more organized. The earth element makes you focused on health and order, and you are known to worry about wellness and can be a hypochondriac. There are times you can be too realistic and critical and it's hard for you to trust things that are too imaginative or emotional. It is important that you control your worry.

Personality Color: Gold

Virgo is a gold personality which enhances your need for routine and structure in order to survive. Unexpected changes can create worry and anxiety. You dislike chaos and crave security. You like things to be structured, planned, and on time. Preparation, order, routine, and efficiency make you feel happy. Disciplined at heart, you are one of the most hardworking signs of the zodiac.

Gold personalities have high standards and can be rigid, strict, and resistant to change. Your critical nature can be used to make things better because you care about others. As an earth sign and a gold personality, you are dependable, responsible, diligent, and organized. Responsibilities are taken seriously, and you don't shy away from hard work.

It is important that you make time for fun, relaxation, and to pursue hobbies. You need to take breaks from work. You can focus too much on tasks and responsibilities leaving little time to enjoy life. Work is not everything; you need a good balance between work, family, and self-care. Being spontaneous is unsettling, you prefer to be dependable and reliable. Other people know they can count on you. When you commit to something you will follow through. You have high expectations for yourself and others. Just remember that no one is perfect.

The Virgo Current Life Relationship Landscape

If you were born under the sign Virgo you are blessed with the power of a strong, analytical mind. Your closest friends and lovers probably depend on your problem-solving ability. Your attention to detail is the envy of the other signs in that you see things others may miss. The traditional astrology phrase for Virgo is "I organize." You can be supportive of those people you care about in unique ways, winning their loyalty.

You enjoy people letting you be yourself. If someone puts you under a microscope you wish they would cut you some slack. Some criticism of you can be tolerated, but if it becomes extreme you tend to tune this out of your mind. When you offer advice and know when to stop giving it, people are open to your suggestions.

You trust those who communicate without hidden agendas. It is then you will do the same for them. You find that people love you more when you don't demand too much perfection from them. If someone becomes too emotionally dependent you will do your best to comfort them. You will look for them to return a shoulder to lean on when you need one.

A lover who does not pressure you to open up your feelings too fast will win your heart. There is an inner strength that you possess that attracts someone who recognizes it. You tend to hide your emotions until a person proves he or she is worthy to have it shown to them.

Some individuals will perceive you as complicated. You see yourself as having your own way of processing life, through a carefully organized mental filter. The more a person gets to know your thought processes the closer they can be to you. Falling in love for you may begin with a few small steps and eventually become a run. When you believe in the potential for a relationship to thrive you are willing to become a solid and committed partner.

The Virgo Past Life Karmic Relationship Patterns

Each of us comes into an incarnation with past life memories. You probably will not find each of the karmic past life patterns discussed as part of your own reality. If one or more seems like part of your way of living in the world, don't get too worried. The information in this book is meant to be a guide to bring greater awareness. You could find a path to empowerment in dealing with a past life pattern.

As a Virgo, your laser-like perceptions may only need a gentle tweak in a new direction to rise above a past life pattern. It takes patience to put new learning into practice. There is no need to judge yourself. There is no race against time, just a new understanding of how to better express the energy in past life patterns. A sense of renewed energy and greater joy is possible in getting a clearer view of a past pattern.

Too Picky

Your sign Virgo gives you a natural tendency to carefully scrutinize which individuals you want as close friends or lovers. It is possible a past life instinct followed you into this incarnation to look for perfection that is impossible to find in a person. If you raise the bar to extreme heights, people will have trouble meeting you halfway in a relationship. This past life pattern can be a defense mechanism to keep people at a distance. Just be sure you aren't too finely sifting through what you think you perceive in someone. It might be your wonderful ability to analyze imperfections in a person that could cause you to miss out on a good relationship.

Another way this pattern could come your way is through a person expecting too much perfection from you. The universe may be showing you the pattern of behavior in someone else to allow you to realize you don't want to repeat this pattern yourself.

Rush to Judgment

This is a past life pattern that will find you doubting the future success of a relationship very fast. This could be a repeating theme in this incarnation that is still an active part of your thought processes. Not giving enough time to develop a relationship with someone might be linked to this pattern. The usual patience of an earth sign like yourself is missing. There are times your intuition will quickly signal that a person is not right for you. That is good in that you make swift decisions to move away from people who would not be positive influences. But if you never really wait long enough to let the depth of a relationship reveal itself, you are likely missing out on a good partnership.

Loss of Hope

This pattern is connected to some past lives where you had self-esteem problems. It impacted on your hopes to find a suitable relationship. You did not feel worthy of receiving love and affection. A negative outlook sometimes attracted the wrong type of partner. If this pattern gets activated in the current incarnation it can cause you to try to fit into relationships that lack harmony. You are denying yourself the chance to choose people with a greater possibility of working toward a happier reality. You will likely be working too hard to keep a relationship afloat if you are too engaged in this pattern.

Mind in the Rear Mirror

There are times you could feel like you have been snagged in the clutches of this past life pattern if you remain fixated on a relationship that did not work. You may be comparing new love interests you meet to a past lover and holding them to unrealistic expectations. It could be that in some past incarnations you suffered a hurtful disappointment in a relationship that prevented you from moving onto a new one. This memory could have come alive again and is blocking your ability to open up your feelings to a new person. It could even be causing tension in an existing relationship if the pattern intensifies. If you are unwilling to let go of a past romance that has no chance of coming back, it makes it difficult to enjoy the promise of a new partner. There is the possibility that you are denying what went wrong in a relationship that has ended. You are only remembering the good from the past encounter and refusing to examine the issues.

Too Much Anxiety

If you are extremely worried about whether you are perfect enough to be in a relationship, you could be reading from a script written by this past life pattern. The perceptive eye you have for detail can turn inward, causing you too much anxiety to commit to a relationship. Virgo is ruled by the planet Mercury, that winged messenger of the gods in mythology. Sometimes your mind may be flying too much, worrying about making mistakes in a relationship. It makes it a real challenge to trust people if you are in the habit of questioning if you have the right tools to be in that relationship. You could be with a very compatible person, but your mental anxiety is bringing a lack of stability into the relationship. The tendency to pull back due to feeling uncomfortable with others is a clue this past life pattern is too prevalent in your life.

Stuck in Routine Thinking

This past life pattern may appear in the form of holding onto your own territory in uncompromising ways. Adapting to the needs of others is not easy if you are fixated on your own routines. Communication is a challenge if you are afraid to leave your comfort zones. You may have great expectation for others to do most of the adjusting in the relationship. Power struggles result on a regular basis if you are too attached to this past pattern of thought and harmony and intimacy will likely seem like out-of-reach strangers. There is an underlying theme of wanting to stay in control. Holding on to old ways of thinking without listening to the ideas of others makes a meeting of minds difficult.

The Critic

You can be very aware of how the actions and words of individuals impact your everyday life. There are times that you may wish that the natural radar you possess to analyze the habits of others was turned off. Occasionally, criticizing the people you are closest with is not going to be a problem. It is if you can't stop being a critic that a great deal of tension manifests. If this past life pattern kicks in strongly, all you see are things you don't like. You might not even realize that you are forgetting to highlight the positives when someone does something you approve of. That Virgo attention to detail can accomplish great things, but putting someone you care about under a microscope too often can get them to react angrily and cause them to pull away.

There is another way this pattern can present itself. It may be a partner or friend that displays this pattern. It might be you have come into this incarnation to drop this behavior and are being presented with a direct view of this pattern coming from someone else. It is your chance to perceive this as a pattern that you don't want to embrace for yourself.

Surrendered Identity

There is a service-oriented instinct in the Virgo sign. It makes others feel at ease in being supportive of their most important goals. This pattern is activated from a past life carryover and causes trouble if your identity is clouded by you trying too hard to make the lives of others a success. Your own plans for the future may get lost in trying to please other individuals. Your assertiveness becomes watered down in not speaking up for your own ideas if this pattern becomes a reality. Your own personal empowerment is being submerged under the thinking you must feed into the power of someone else. The equality in a relationship is missing, keeping you in a subservient role.

Extreme Worrying

If this past life pattern is a frequent visitor it can get you to over think how you relate to people. You are expecting too much perfection from yourself in unrealistic ways. That great power to analyze, if pointed inward in an obsessive tendency, can result in too much negative thinking. You can be trying to please everyone all of the time. Being afraid to make a mistake is often at the root system of this pattern lurking in past life memories. A fear of stepping out of this pattern keeps you trapped in it. The fulfillment you are in search of in a relationship stays out of your reach until you walk away from this shadowy energy.

I Am Not Deserving

Giving out love and affection but not being comfortable with receiving this from others is an indication this past life pattern has some sway over you. It could be you don't feel worthy of a fulfilling relationship. It is possible you are in a good, rewarding romance or friendship but still resist accepting the fact you deserve love. Some past lives that lacked the emotional warmth you wanted may be interfering with trusting the love coming your way in this incarnation. Those people closest to you may sense you tighten up when they try to reward you with positive support and compliments. Finding your way to accept the intimacy and love you deserve in this life is the challenge.

Denying Anger

A clue this past life pattern has emerged into your current incarnation is if you are too timid in expressing anger. This will likely create some intense moods you don't want to feel. Your perceptions about people may become clouded by an inner emotional intensity due to bottled up anger. Rather than dealing with a tense situation in the present, you will be drained of energy by carrying around hurt feelings. There is some truth that taking some downtime before overreacting to a situation might be wise. But if you are repeatedly hiding your opposition to someone else's behavior, eventually you could explode more than you wanted to. It is very possible that in some past lives you dealt with anger by not expressing it for fear of someone's reaction. Your memory of these lives could be influencing your thinking in this life.

Ruled by Guilt

This past life pattern is a reenactment from incarnations that found you feeling too responsible for the problems of others. You were blamed too much of the time for mistakes being made by other people. In this life you could become the scapegoat again if you give in to guilt. Taking on too much responsibility to bail people out of trouble they created begins to wear you out. The harmony you long for is being swallowed up by losing sight of your boundaries.

Another way this past life pattern exposes itself is by individuals who know how to push your guilt buttons. They are manipulating you into a guilt trap. It is an opportunity to say no, that you can't go back into a pattern you came into this incarnation to avoid. If you deny you are doing favors for others out of guilt, this past life influence will ensnare you.

The Virgo Reward for Using Your Sixth Sense Intuitive Perception to Solve Karmic Relationship Patterns

Your mind will feel like it has been given a wonderful recharge when gaining clarity about a past life pattern. It may even feel like the shadow force of a karmic pattern never really had any control over you. The harmony you want to enjoy in your relationships will seem much easier to attain. It is an empowering feeling to escape the hold of a pattern of behavior that was interfering with your happiness.

There is nothing to fear if any of the past life patterns that have been discussed sound familiar. The main thing to remember is that in acknowledging a pattern, you can begin to move in a new direction. Taking what was a limiting or negative energy into a more positive expression is liberating. The insight you gain in facing a past life energy can give you enlightened eyes to find the fulfillment you seek in relationships and other areas of your life. It is a learning process that takes some practice to move past any karmic pattern. There is no need to judge yourself if you identify with any of the patterns discussed. The key thing to remember is that in taking those initial steps to bring a past life pattern into clearer focus, it can allow you the love you hope to experience.

If the Too Picky past life pattern seems like too big a part of your perceptions of people it might be a lingering energy from past incarnations. You need to have as a mantra that there are no perfect people. What you are viewing as imperfection in someone could be their uniqueness. Letting yourself go beyond your comfort zone allows you to interact with individuals that may be a good match for you. Sometimes being open to differences in one another makes a relationship stimulating. You could need to accept a person the way they are, in the same way you hope to be treated by them. There is nothing wrong with being careful in who you allow to get to know you in an intimate way. But if you are too narrow in the type of person you think you need to be happy, it does limit your options. The happiness and harmony you want in a relationship is closer than you think. It may only take altering your expectations slightly to bring into reality a very fulfilling partnership.

There is an inner restless energy that can manifest in the Rush to Judgment pattern. If this past life shadow force is too prevalent in your current life, there is a tendency to move impatiently away from relationships. Taking the time to get to really know someone may prove rewarding. Steering away from jumping to conclusions about people lessens the intensity of this past life pattern. If you slow down, you could enjoy having a person in your life who supports your goals and is there for you during a challenging period. The hold of this pattern is less likely if you realize that the potential for a relationship to be fulfilling needs time to develop. If you grow comfortable in patiently communicating your needs to someone, you can find your way out of this pattern's influence.

In the Loss of Hope pattern you have to put yourself first, even if it feels strange to do so. You will find it will bring this past life energy into balance. The tendency to serve others is in the DNA of your Virgo sign. People in some past lives likely took advantage of your generosity. You came into this life to make sure you did not go overboard in pleasing others. You will find, in making sure your own identity and goals are being supported by people you are close to, that your relationships begin walking down harmony lane. It will be faster than you might think to overcome this pattern if you remember to check in with yourself and to make sure you are being recognized as an equal.

The Mind in the Rear View Mirror does take some retraining of your mind to look forward rather than back to the past. Letting go of a past relationship allows the possibility of being with someone that meets the needs of who you are in the present. Weaning yourself away from the memory of what you think was a person you can't live without, slowly releases a new, revitalized energy in you. In releasing the past, the universe often responds with a magical synchronicity to bring new individuals into our life with a similar desire for a fulfilling relationship. Keeping your focus on the here and now awakens the future with more rewarding options.

The Too Much Anxiety pattern can be overcome through staying away from unnecessary worry about things you can't control. There is a wonderful ability in Virgo to be a careful planner. Sometimes a relationship gets messy because nobody is perfect. If you let go of the fear of making mistakes in a relationship, you will be happier and find a greater level of comfort in being with someone. You may find that your closest friends and loved ones don't expect the impossible from you. Taking the pressure of unrealistic expectations off of yourself paves the way for happiness and fulfillment. Having a regular routine that channels nervous energy away from you could relax your mind, to keep away the tendency to over worry.

The Stuck in Routine Thinking pattern can be conquered by being open to new ideas. It often is comforting for a Virgo like yourself to stick to what works for you. If you are flexible it helps maintain harmony in your relationships. There is a capacity to adapt to change in your sign. When you make use of this ability, people are more likely to be supportive of your important goals. Being willing to step out of your comfort zones does keep this pattern in check. Love and fulfillment come to you faster when you let go of a need to keep life too predictable. You give the universe an opportunity to surprise you with rewarding relationships when you aren't too resistant to new perceptions.

The Critic pattern only needs you to point the awareness you have toward a positive direction. You may find it easier than you might think to convert this past life influence into a more favorable experience. If you focus on what someone is doing right in your opinion, they may begin to change a behavior you find annoying. Positive support given to those people you care about is a sure path to creating harmony. Being a Virgo adorns you with valuable insights into the minds of others. Working harder on the issues rather than trying to change someone is a bridge to greater fulfillment with that person.

It can also be true that you don't have to accept being a regular target of criticism. If you regularly attract individuals into your life who act out this pattern, then the universe is trying to make you aware that this is not an energy you want to adopt. Sometimes a past life pattern we once were in the habit of using comes to us through someone else. It is a chance to be vigilant to guard against accepting this as part of your own thought processes.

The Surrendered Identity pattern is balanced by not forgetting to nourish the goals that inspire your mind and soul. It truly is the way to go beyond the reach of this pattern if it should try to influence you. Virgo is an earth sign which means you need to stay grounded to your own unique path. It is from here that you have much to offer, without losing yourself in the life of someone else. Love is a wonderful thing that you enjoy more when being true to your own needs. It is easier to be there for people you care about when you are tuned into your own identity. Your intuition, mind and emotions function from a very high level when expressing yourself from a clear connection to your identity. Others benefit when they show recognition of your own unique gifts.

The Extreme Worrying past life pattern has a pathway from which to escape. The challenge is finding it. One of the keys to the trail leading away from this past life influence is not being afraid to make mistakes. There are no perfect people or relationships. You probably need to take the pressure of unrealistic expectations off of you. This will take great tension away from how you relate to others. The intimacy you hope to experience is easier to accomplish when you don't try to be too perfect. You will more comfortably adjust to a relationship when not becoming preoccupied with trying to do everything just right. It might take some practice for not worrying to become a natural component of how you engage in a relationship, but it is well worth the effort.

The I Am Not Deserving pattern is asking you to change your attitude about receiving compliments and affection. It gives a smoother flow to your sharing in relationships when you are open to receiving as much as giving. You will find people are more receptive to the love you give when allowing yourself to be a receiver. Trusting to take small steps to be more open emotionally deepens the bond you will experience with someone. This may take getting beyond a fear to let someone know you on a deeper level but the fulfillment awaiting you will be a great reward.

The Denying Anger past life pattern will become a distant type of influence if you get better at letting your feelings be known. Emotional intensity is usually linked to the passion you want to express in letting your voice be heard. Cutting through layers of past life memories where your ideas were held back can be overcome by being more assertive. Your relationships find balance if you are more direct in being yourself. When you take steps to be in the moment with honest communication, there is less need to have anger building within you. The energy it takes to hide anger can be channeled into more productive directions. Sometimes it is the fear of letting anger out that needs to be overcome. You might be surprised that anger can bring people closer as it brings a problem out into the open so it can be solved.

The Ruled by Guilt pattern is playing off of an instinct you have to fix the problems other people have created. If you learn to set limits on how much you can take on for others, this past life pattern will not be a problem. Your energy levels and emotional strength are stronger when being reasonable in helping people. You are a more reliable friend, family member and lover when not allowing a feeling of guilt to rule you. Performing actions not based on guilt empowers your relationships.

Another way to resolve this pattern is by listening to your intuition when it is telling you not to embrace guilt. Eventually you will get good at perceiving individuals who seem to know how to manipulate you through guilt. Stopping this past life pattern from occurring is liberating. Trusting your perceptions to let them guide you away from walking in the footsteps of guilt is your path out of this past life pattern.

The Virgo Reward from Solving Karmic Patterns

You have the tenacity embedded in your mind to work your way through any past life pattern. Think of it as starting a new project when it comes to walking on the path of overcoming any pattern you want to change. Each step you take will lead to more confident ones as you move away from the hold of a pattern. The result is you will notice your relationships will have greater flow. Communication between you and your closest allies will likely become clearer. Your sense of personal power will grow stronger in coming to grips with a pattern. Your tendency to act out a past life pattern will lessen with patience and practice.

If any of the patterns discussed sound familiar don't worry. Remember that first you have to perceive a behavior before you can change it. You need not feel any pressure to change a past life pattern overnight. If you use that Virgo determination to rise above a pattern's influence, you will come out the winner.

Don't make perfection your goal. Rather see your efforts in dealing with past life influences as a road to greater relationship fulfillment. The harmony and peace you hope to achieve is within your grasp in beginning the journey of self-discovery.

Virgo the Sage Journal Prompts

1. How do you feel when you see the Virgo image?
2. What Virgo archetype traits do you resonate most with?
3. Are you a worrier or do you experience anxiety?
4. In what areas of life are you a perfectionist?
5. How do you take care of your diet, health, and body?
6. What do you do to relax, reduce stress, and find solitude?
7. What past life patterns have you experienced?

Chapter Seven

Libra the Lover

"I COMPROMISE"
Keywords: Balanced, Charming, Artistic, Diplomatic, Indecisive, Attractive
Sun Sign Dates: September 22–October 22
Temperament: Sanguine
Sign Type: Air, Cardinal
Planetary Ruler: Venus
Jungian Archetype: The Lover
Tarot Card: Justice
Polar Opposite Archetype: The Hero
Astrology Nickname: The Peacemaker
Polar Opposite Sign: Aries
Symbol: The Scales
Personality Color: Green, Extroverted
Rules: The Seventh House, the Kidneys, Back

Libra Temperament: Sanguine

Libra is the seventh sign of the zodiac. You are intelligent and curious about learning. You are ruled by the scales of balance, so you often change your mind. Indecisiveness can cause problems in relationships. It is difficult for you to deal with conflict because you want to make other people happy. Even though you are charming, creative, and artistic there is a side of you that can be distant and shy. Sometimes due to a reserved nature, people might think you don't like them. Libra is similar to the sanguine temperament. There is an adaptability and easygoing part of you that attracts other people. This temperament makes you hesitant, confused, and conflict-avoidant which makes it hard to make decisions for your own life. Prioritizing harmony can make you suppress your true feelings. Being diplomatic comes naturally to you because you are a peacemaker. You are people-oriented and find your identity through relationships. Sanguine energy is similar to air energy and intensifies your need for social connections and learning new things.

Trying to balance everything and pretending to be happy even when you are not, can lead other people to perceive you as superficial. You are not fake, but your avoidance of deep emotions can make those closest to you feel uncomfortable. They can sense that you are holding back, and it can cause communication problems. Most sanguine personalities can be impulsive and scattered mentally. You can feel this way sometimes but because of your ability to balance your thoughts and emotions you find stability. Your strength is your ability to help other people be more grounded. As a Libra, you bring a sense of support to those around you, and they know that you care about their needs.

Jungian Archetype: The Lover

Libra is associated with the lover archetype. It is no surprise that you are the lover because your planetary ruler is Venus. Venus is all about love, beauty, and relationships. Your sign rules the seventh house of marriage and partnership in astrology. Finding someone to love and depend on is an important part of your journey. You are focused on making other people happy and are an excellent mediator. Keeping relationships peaceful and harmonious is critical for your emotional well-being. You are flirtatious and enjoy affection when you are in a relationship. Commitment and being able to depend on others to take care of you helps you find security. One downside of being the lover archetype is that you might be uncomfortable being alone. You might jump from relationship to relationship and be indecisive.

You might feel restless and lonely if you are not in some sort of relationship. Sometimes you're indecisive about relationships and find it hard to break things off with someone who is not compatible with you. You dislike being alone and like spending time with others. Learning to balance love and relationships will be one of your most challenging lessons.

Tarot Card Archetype: Justice

Libra's symbol is the metal scales of balance. The Justice card symbolizes the need for you to ensure fairness and equilibrium. Truth, justice, and equality for all embody your moral compass. As a Libra, your goal is to balance your emotions and thoughts. You might be attracted to careers in law, criminal justice, coaching, and teaching. You have a natural ability to help others see both sides of an issue and compromise. Putting other people's needs before your own comes naturally, but you must not allow others to walk all over you. Standing up for the underdog and supporting others is where you shine. Just don't forget to speak up for your own rights and needs, especially in relationships. In this card you can see the scales of balance and the sword representing the air element. As a Libra there is a deep need to judge the actions of others and to ensure peace, harmony, fairness, and balance in all areas of life.

Element: Air

Libra is an air sign, and you are known to be both intellectual and artistic. You are a peacemaker and avoid conflict. Social and easygoing, it's easy for you to make friends. Venus is your ruling planet, and it gives you a more romantic side than most other air signs. You like to learn new things and study. Even though you like being in love, there is also a side of your personality that wants to feel free. Many air signs want to have independence, but you are actually seeking interdependence. Having a relationship partner and someone to spend time with brings fulfillment. Because your sign rules the house of partnership you do best when you are with other people. Being alone won't be easy for you. You can be flirtatious, social, outgoing, and friendly. Then other times you can be introverted and find it difficult to talk with others. You are intelligent but you need a career field that helps you tap into your creative ideas.

Personality Color: Green

Libras are similar to green personalities. Both are intellectual and have a creative mind. You value information, facts, figures, and knowledge. You might feel uncomfortable making choices based on emotions. You prefer to study and research things before you make a decision. You enjoy relationships and can be friendly and flirtatious. Sometimes aloof and emotionally distant, you can confuse others. As a green personality you tend to overthink and enjoy your freedom. You can rebel if you feel smothered or controlled. You like being friends with many different types of people and need a partner that gives you space when you need it. Communicating and sharing ideas is an important part of your life. You like to help other people solve problems and find peaceful solutions. You can be indecisive because you are open-minded and want to be understanding about many different points of views.

The Libra Current Life Relationship Landscape

If you were born under the sign of Libra you have a natural way of making others feel at ease. Your personality is outgoing, especially if you are comfortable with social situations. The traditional astrology phrase for Libra is "I balance." Keeping your own emotions and mental energies in balance is important to your sense of comfort. You appreciate people who are not overly demanding of your generosity. Individuals who know how to surprise you with pleasant experiences excite you.

Those who infringe on your time can wear you out unless they are near and dear to your heart.

Romantic atmospheres are a way to your most intimate feelings. You long for a soul mate with similar interests. There will be certain goals or pastimes you need your lovers to support. If they appreciate your unique ideas, you will be a friend for life. You like to know that people are listening when you speak. If you feel discounted it arouses your anger quickly. You will hide your emotions from someone until you are sure they are deserving to have them revealed.

Some people may perceive you as hard to please. You probably see this as having particular likes and dislikes that are not out of the ordinary. You will be patient to let a relationship develop. On the other hand, you will pull back if a person gives you a good reason to no longer trust them.

You value partnership. There is an inner desire to want those important people in your life to be patient with you. You are likely to have a wide variety of acquaintances. Receiving input of new ideas from all different types of individuals opens your eyes to greater options to realize your future goals.

The Libra Past Life Karmic Relationship Patterns

Everyone has brought past life patterns into the current life. It might make you feel better to know you are not alone. If you connect with one or more of the past life patterns discussed here, don't let it worry you. In acknowledging that a karmic theme has been part of your current incarnation, you are taking the first steps to transform the energy into a more productive expression. It does take patience to work your way through past life influences that might be interfering with your relationship fulfillment. Think of the effort you make to discover better ways to make use of past life energy as a way to have a happier and more abundant life.

As a Libra, your passion to seek a balanced life can persuade any past life energy to work in favorable directions. Your dedication in wanting a relationship filled with harmony will keep you on the right path. If you notice you are slipping back into the web of a past life pattern, don't get frustrated. Each time you start again to make peace with shadow forces from past lives, your insights will guide you to see the world with a renewed vision. When you release a past life pattern the road ahead is filled with the people you long to meet that share your dreams and need for love.

Sitting on the Fence

If this past life pattern has become too activated in your current life, it produces a great amount of indecision when it comes to settling into a relationship. Libra is known for weighing decisions on a scale. There is nothing wrong with carefully contemplating if someone is right for you. The conflict does become a reality in this pattern if it causes you to fear making a commitment. It could be that in some past lives a repeating theme was never finding a sense of comfort as relationships grew closer. Usually, the culprit in this pattern gaining influence is not being able to trust others. It may be not believing enough in yourself to sustain a relationship that requires emotional depth. This is not saying that you acted this way in all of your past lives, only the ones linked to this pattern.

I Am Lost Without You

This past life pattern, when it becomes too dominant, causes an extreme dependency on others. The real problem comes if you are too attached to someone to not pay attention to your own needs. The boundaries become very blurred to the point where you can feel like you are serving the life of someone else and neglecting your own. It is painful for a Libra to be in a partnership that feels like a partner is too invisible when it comes to not getting the emotional support you desire. Your resources are getting poured into a person who isn't returning the favor. Your goals can become distracted by the worry you feel in not getting the reassurance that someone is really there for you. If you stay in a state of denial about the reality of the relationship it begins to drain you on both mental and emotional levels.

Too Compromising

As a Libra you have a natural instinct to try to create fairness in your negotiations with others. If this past life pattern emerges, you can find yourself going too far in trying to please people. This is especially true in your closest relationships. Emotions have a way of fogging your perceptions when you are afraid of disappointing someone. If you give much more than you receive to keep a person close to you, it might begin to throw a relationship out of balance. It could be a fear of causing anger if you disagree with a partner that keeps this pattern hovering over you. Tiptoeing around sensitive issues in your relationships is a type of behavior that compromises how you really feel. The result causes more problems than handling differences in a direct manner. The price you are paying grows bigger when you enable others to expect you to be overly accommodating.

Winning At All Costs

This is a pattern that becomes too operational in your life if you lose sight of opposing points of view. Being challenged is perceived as a threat by you. It becomes too important to push your own ideas, creating extreme tension in your communication with others. The love and intimacy you hope for become absent. This carryover from some of your past life experiences puts you on the defense probably more than needed. A fear of becoming too vulnerable is another way this past life pattern enters the current life. You don't want to show any weakness, but you could be pushing away individuals that would make good lovers or friends.

Another way this pattern might manifest is through people you know. You are getting a chance to observe how this pattern you once displayed in past lives is working in someone else's. The challenge is not walking backward into this pattern again by being pulled into it by someone ensnared by this pattern in their own life.

Too Aloof

Libra is an air sign which accentuates the intellectual side of life. This pattern can weave its way into your current incarnation if you too often allow your intellect to hide your emotions. The tricky thing about this pattern is that you could be completely unaware you are repeating a past life scenario. The closest people in your life might perceive you as purposely not wanting to show your feelings. You may rationalize this as needing to stay mentally clear. The problem here is that you might seem uncaring when a person you care about needs emotional support. The intimacy and love you want to receive could be held back by a loved one if they can't connect with your inner world. Your comfort in communicating intellectual words and concepts has trouble in transferring over to your cerebral circuitry that deals with feelings. In your own mind you may think you are expressing yourself adequately while someone close to you perceives you to be miles away.

Loss of Identity

As a Libra you thrive on your people connections. This past life pattern works its way into your current life if you depend too much on someone else to confirm your identity. It could be you are attracting friends and lovers with strong personalities that overly influence your goals. Your ideas get water thrown on them too much of the time. You might experience some confusion in defining what you really need from others to be happy. The assertion to speak with a confident voice is negated by those with louder ones. Giving into who people think you should be rather than being yourself makes you feel like a stranger in a strange land. Accepting negative messages about yourself from manipulative individuals keeps the harmony you long for away from you. You came into this life to walk away from this pattern but the portal out of this past memory remains a mystery.

Future Goal Confusion

If this past life pattern becomes active in your life you can be living too much through the goals of others. There may be a tendency to think you have to have the same future plans as those closest to you. A self-imposed peer pressure may be overly influencing your ideas about your future plans. The template others are using to define what they want from life has been superimposed on your own thoughts. A sense of stagnation can take place until you tune into your own authentic needs. It isn't that you lack inner strength as much as you need to align with your own passion. This pattern might find you overthinking rather than taking action. You could be too sensitive in letting the insights that work for others block your own.

Rigid Strategist

Libra is blessed with a strategy-oriented mind that can become a great focus to accomplishing a plan. This pattern occurs when you can't adapt to the goals of others to develop a shared path to success. It could be that in some past lives you felt a need to hold on to your own ideas at all costs. Your memory of those lives is embedded in your consciousness but does not mean you have to act out this pattern of reasoning again. Your relationships will endure great tension if you are too attached to a strategy that can't allow you to hear what others need from you. Having mental toughness can be a true asset. But seeing the world through a fixed mindset makes it a challenge for people to get close to you. This pattern creates the likelihood that you will stimulate the differences between you and someone rather than finding a road that leads to harmony.

Fear of Commitment

If this past life pattern makes its presence known, you could show a reluctance to let yourself get serious about a relationship. A challenge in trusting that you have found the right person for yourself could be a repeating event. You may like the idea of finding a soul mate but have trouble believing in the reality of finding a special person. Partnership is likely meaningful to you, as is friendship. The more emotional you start to become about a person, you suddenly hit the brakes. This is a past life pattern lodged in your memory that if activated blocks you from falling in love. This pattern may be linked to a feeling of divine discontent that has you thinking there should be a perfect person waiting for you to discover. This can't occur because nobody is perfect.

Another possible appearance of this pattern is that it approaches you in the form of someone else displaying this behavior. This is your opportunity to perceive this influence in another individual but not to act out this shadow force yourself. In other words, you came into this life to sidestep this karmic expression.

Ruled by Anxiety

Your sign Libra belongs to the intellectually-oriented air element. Your mental circuitry at times becomes overloaded if you feel you are getting too much input from people. Your nervous system intensifies in close relationships if individuals appear to be leaning on you too heavily for their emotional needs. You may suddenly need to pull away to get your objectivity back. This past life pattern surfaces more when you don't take some space to reclaim your clear thinking. Your moods grow stronger when not getting occasional alone time. Your emotional intensity could explode if you feel too pressured into making decisions. Having a strong intellect is in the DNA of your sign. If you don't claim your own space in a relationship your mental energy gets weaker. This past life pattern gains in strength if you don't realize you can't always be expected to solve someone else's problems.

Starved for Attention

Being born under a people-oriented sign like Libra can bring you to want to have your voice heard by a wide range of individuals. It is when the drive for attention grows compulsive that this past life pattern gets activated. There might be a feeling you are being ignored by those people you are the closest to on a regular basis, no matter how much admiration you receive. This is a sign that this past life pattern has come alive. There is nothing wrong with wanting to have your own ideas recognized and supported by those you care about. Usually, this pattern has its roots in feelings of a deep insecurity. There may have been past lives where you were overly taken for granted. In those past incarnations, your opinions may not have been valued. It is possible that in the current life the scale has tipped too far in compulsively feeling a need for attention. You can keep asking individuals to prove over and over again that they truly care about you, no matter how much they are already doing this. This is a pattern that can throw cold water on the warm intimacy you hope to have in relationships.

Masquerade

Each of us has a persona or mask we show to the public. It is our personal style and our way of socializing. This past life pattern becomes a problem if you depend too much on presenting an image of yourself to others but never get beyond it. It keeps you from true intimacy and a deeper emotional connection with someone. This pattern is not an issue in casual encounters. The interference from this past life pattern causes trouble in the relationships you want to explore on a deeper level. There is a playful side of this pattern. It is only when you can't come out of the shadows of this past influence into the light, revealing more of your inner world, that you can miss out on a good relationship. You are likely having trouble trusting yourself and others enough to release the hold of this pattern of thinking.

The Libra Reward for Using Your Sixth Sense Intuitive Perception to Solve Karmic Relationship Patterns

The weight lifted off of your mind in letting go of a karmic pattern is wonderful. Your positive thinking about people could rise to a higher level. Your self-confidence to embark in a new relationship direction can get ignited. Trusting your insights about others may become stronger. Whatever was a past life memory block opens up new, stimulating energy. Giving and receiving love could feel more flowing. There is no turning back once you have removed yourself out of the line of fire from a pattern of behavior that was interfering with your happiness.

There is a likelihood that at least one of the past life patterns discussed hit the mark with your own experiences. If this is true, don't judge yourself. Nothing here is intended to shine a negative light on you. Memories from past lives that are not beneficial for this lifetime take practice and much patience to channel into a positive expression. Those first steps into a new direction might feel awkward. It is like learning new perceptions that elevate your insight to better grasp the awareness to navigate through a past life energy. Think of it as bringing thought patterns out of the shadows into a new illuminating light. It is an opportunity to embrace a journey of self-discovery that can reward you with fulfilling relationship harmony.

The Sitting on the Fence pattern is sometimes easier to handle if you take the risk of letting someone get to know you on a deeper level. If this past life influence is a regular occurrence in your life, it will take some determination to get more decisive. There is nothing to really fear. Often the indecision about a person is more frustrating than giving a relationship a chance to evolve. It does take time for a relationship to reveal itself. The love you want to share with someone does require being willing to face adversity. Every relationship takes some adjusting to one another's needs. The trust you need to have in yourself may be closer than you think. Love in many ways takes a leap of faith. There is probably a side of you that believes in reality-testing a partnership. You could be using this pragmatism too early in getting to know someone. If you view a relationship as a process that will unfold naturally, it could allow you to jump off the fence.

The I Am Lost Without You pattern will stop surfacing if you break the attachment to supporting someone else's life to the exclusion of your own. It will probably seem awkward as you put yourself first. You might even accuse yourself of being selfish, but it will take this to get your life back into balance. When you begin to put yourself into relationships that give you a feeling of equality, it is a rebirth. You are reclaiming your power and finding new vitality on the road to personal empowerment. You may have attracted controlling types of people in past lives and need to be vigilant in this life not to allow it to happen again. As you focus in a new direction, this pattern will seem like something from the distant past. In finding a greater sense of you there is less likelihood in getting lost in someone else.

The Too Compromising pattern reveals you might need to put a stop in being too ready to give in to the demands of others. Your negotiating skills need to get stronger. If you can get past the worry of causing friction because you openly stand up for your opinions, you are at least halfway in leaving this past life pattern behind. People who truly want to develop a relationship based on a mutual sharing of power, will not expect you to do all of the compromising. When you get over a reluctance to be assertive, your relationships fall into a natural balance. The desire to seek fairness in your social interactions is a Libra trait. You will attract individuals with a similar quest for equality as you value having this in your relationships. If you perceive the need to be uncompromising when it comes to being treated as an equal partner in major decisions, this pattern will let go of you.

The Winning At All Costs pattern can be turned away from a negative expression by tapping into that Libra strategic ability you possess to create win-win results. Rather than expending immense amounts of energy fighting constantly for your point of view, it is more productive to try to reach shared resolutions. Sometimes agreeing to disagree is another way to lessen the likelihood of this past life influence coming into your life. Creating enough ground for you and others to be mutually supportive of goals is one of your strengths. Focusing your mental energy to pursue your dreams gets the support you want to receive when you do the same for others. It is great to passionately fight for your ideas. If you don't lose sight of the voice of those you care about, the harmony you cherish is never far away. Truly listening to someone as you state your case in a dispute puts this past life pattern to rest.

The Too Aloof pattern can be overcome by allowing your emotional world to be discovered by others. You have a well-developed mental strength that only needs to let your feelings be expressed. Your lovers and friends want to come closer when your emotions are visible. It may be that you need to trust that appearing vulnerable to someone you love makes the intimacy stronger. Having the courage to reveal your inner world puts you in the driver's seat in overcoming this past life influence. It might be you think talking on an intellectual level is revealing enough. If you can accept the feedback from someone, that they need you to communicate your feelings, then this pattern weakens in its intensity. The path to greater fulfillment in your relationships is in the here and now, when you begin talking with emotion as well as with your intellect.

The Loss of Identity pattern can get a course correction by not letting others talk you out of your goals. To confirm your identity, you need to trust your mental insights and intuitive instincts. Learning how to decipher the input you get from others, and separating what is useful from what is negating your self-image puts you out in front of this pattern. You came into this life to stand up for your ideas. It is okay to let someone's advice help guide you. Just be sure in the end it is your own inner voice that has the last word. If you stop letting opinions from others who are trying to manipulate your thinking from occurring, the result is your identity gets empowered. When you don't try to copy the life of someone else you stay away from the reach of this past life pattern. It is okay to have individuals with strong personalities in your life. They can be uplifting and encourage you to accomplish great things. You only need to be sure to walk to the beat of your own inspirational insights to be true to your own identity.

The Future Goal Confusion pattern only needs you to align with your own inspirational thinking. It is a good thing to take into consideration advice you are given by others. You will become empowered when making choices that reflect your own values and needs. When you live out your own goals, you are giving the universe more ways to offer you greater opportunities for abundance. The power of attracting relationships with a promise of fulfillment creates a magical synchronicity when you launch out in independent directions. You will find that your partnerships and friendships benefit from making choices that emanate from your own passion. There is a chance this past life pattern has been hidden from your conscious mind. When you express your most authentic ideas for the future, this pattern will stay out of your current life.

When you reach out to that balanced objectivity embedded in the fabric of Libra, the Rigid Strategist pattern becomes less likely to appear. You have an excellent ability, like a gifted chess player, to plan a few moves ahead in your thought processes. If you make it clear to others your way of perceiving situations, it makes for greater possibility of winning support. If you show you are listening and are willing to budge from your positions, people become more agreeable. It only takes a spirit of cooperation that allows your friends and lovers to climb on board with you. Giving your strategic advice when requested brings your special people closer. Sometimes it will be your allowing others access to your way of reasoning that takes the tension out of disputes. Remember that Libra is a mentally-oriented air sign that needs to show you care about the feelings of others. It could be your emotional expression that lets others know you hear their voice right alongside your own that is the road to harmony.

The Fear of Commitment pattern comes down to trusting that you deserve a fulfilling relationship. That usually is the first step to rising above the hold of this past life influence. A close intimate relationship with someone may feel like less of a risk as you believe in what you have to offer a partner. Love can get messy as you go through the good and difficult times with a person. If you stay long enough in a relationship, it could reveal the happiness you hope to find. It is very possible, if this pattern is active in your life, that it is linked to some past lives where you felt betrayed in some way. It does not mean it has to happen again. If you stay positive and define clearly what you need from a relationship, this pattern's influence will lessen in a big way. If you don't worry about the commitment but pay attention to getting to know someone, it is a wiser path to follow. Think of being with a person as a journey of self-exploration as much as figuring out if you have found the right person. The mutual acceptance of each other may take some time, so enjoy each step of the path.

You may be attracting people who have commitment issues. It might be an opportunity to get a glimpse of a pattern you don't want to repeat in the current incarnation. It is the universe reminding you that it is a behavior you don't want to fall into.

The Ruled by Anxiety past life pattern is easier to manage if you don't take on too much responsibility in solving the problems of others. You stay mentally and emotionally stable when functioning as a reliable support system with clear boundaries. Your happiness in love and friendship rests upon having realistic expectations for yourself. You can't save someone from facing their own issues. Your relationships will stay in balance if you don't enable others to lean on you without their putting in their own effort. You have valuable insights to share with those closest to you. When you have an equal footing in a relationship, this pattern has less of a chance to appear. There will be occasions when you will need alone time to gather your thoughts. It is an innate need of being a Libra to know when to walk to your own drumbeat and when to take footsteps close together with someone you love.

The Starved for Attention past life pattern might not be as easy to identify from your past life memories. It can hide out of sight from your conscious awareness. It is important to realize you are a complete person without someone else. It is from here that you can create the type of relationship that brings you fulfillment. Harmony with someone is closer than you might think. When you stay grounded in knowing, you don't need another individual to complete you and how you relate to others finds balance. Your sign thrives on partnerships that have a well-established equality. A barometer to know you have the right people in your life is that they don't want all of your attention. They will encourage your independence as much as wanting you to support their own unique goals. Paying attention to your own self-discovery attracts from the universe the relationships that bring you great harmony.

The Masquerade past life pattern only needs you to not be afraid to let others discover you on a deeper level. If you take the challenge of trusting someone, you could be surprised how good it feels. The intimacy and closeness rise fast in your relationships when you reveal more of yourself emotionally. Your ability to be a strong partner for someone makes you highly desirable in the eyes of many others. People really would like to know what lies behind the intellect you display. You don't need to rush yourself to open up if it is difficult. But taking the first step to express feelings as well as your intellect is a winning formula to put this past life pattern to rest.

The Libra Reward from Solving Karmic Patterns

You will feel a great sense of accomplishment when facing a karmic past life influence and rising above it. It is a great relief to do so as it frees you to experience more harmony in your relationships. It is okay if you are only beginning to take the first steps on this journey. Sometimes it is in becoming aware of any of these past life patterns that opens your eyes to new ways to express this energy. The shadow forces embedded in a pattern do come out into the light of clarity when you show you recognize the potential of channeling the energy into productive directions.

It is in your Libra grasp to handle the challenges presented by a past life pattern. You have a level-headedness to navigate your way to a clear understanding of how to disengage from the power of influences that are interfering with the harmony you seek in relationships.

There is a decisiveness within you to transcend a past life pattern with a patient persistence. There is no competition to worry about in getting past a pattern; this is your own journey. Think of it as a self-discovery to create a wonderful highway to find your way to relationship fulfillment.

Libra the Lover Journal Prompts

1. How do you feel when you see the Libra image?
2. What Libra archetype traits do you resonate most with?
3. Are you a peacemaker in your relationships?
4. In what areas of life do you avoid conflict?
5. Do you have artistic talents?
6. What type of partner are you attracted to?
7. What past life patterns have you experienced?

Chapter Eight

Scorpio the Magician

"I PERCEIVE"
Keywords: "Intense, Passionate, Loyal, Determined, Secretive, Deep, Powerful
Sun Sign Dates: October 22–November 21
Temperament: Phlegmatic
Sign Type: Water, Fixed
Planetary Ruler: Pluto
Jungian Archetype: The Magician
Tarot Card: Death
Polar Opposite Archetype: The Real Person
Astrology Nickname: The Phoenix
Polar Opposite Sign: Taurus
Symbol: The Scorpion
Personality Color: Blue, Introverted
Rules: The Eighth House, the Reproductive and Elimination System

Scorpio Temperament: Phlegmatic

Scorpio is the eighth sign of the zodiac. You are associated with the phlegmatic personality type. Still waters run deep. You are emotional, intense, and secretive. There is a magnetic energy that attracts people into your life. There is a private side to your personality. You are able to get other people to tell you their secrets, but you don't fully share your personal problems with others. It takes a lot of time for you to trust others, but once you trust you are extremely loyal.

As a phlegmatic personality it is important to have deep, loyal, and trusting relationships. You are perceptive and psychic and seem to understand the darker side of life. Taboo topics such as death, sex, and occultism fascinate you. People like to share their secrets and problems with you. You have a healing energy that attracts and comforts others. You can have an interest in psychology and learning the mysteries of the universe. Finding an emotional balance and allowing yourself to be open with others can be challenging. You possess a strength that most people are afraid of. People are either very attracted to you or they might feel uncomfortable. Your ability to read people and know their true motives is a spiritual gift. You are powerful and power itself is something you are learning to control. Forgiving others and letting go of the past can help you transform into a stronger person. You're a resilient soul that can help people with your practical and realistic approach.

Jungian Archetype: The Magician

Scorpio is associated with the Magician archetype. You have the ability to rise from the ashes like a phoenix and transform. Mystical and mysterious, it's no wonder that you share similar personality traits with the Magician. You have an interest in metaphysical knowledge such as occultism, astrology, energy healing, and other new age topics. There is a chance that you have a connection to death and the other side. You might even have mediumship abilities. You have a psychological understanding of the cycles of life. Tapping into this powerful energy can help you overcome traumatic and painful life experiences. There is strength that lies deep within that you are able to tap into when you need courage. You have a penetrating gaze that can peek deep inside someone's soul. Others are either drawn to you or are a bit afraid of you. In relationships you want all or nothing. You expect total honesty and loyalty from the people you care about. There is a focused, obsessive, and disciplined part of your personality that does not give up. Just like the Magician, you are able to manifest and tap into the powerful energy of the universe.

Tarot Card Archetype: Death

Scorpio is associated with the tarot card of Death. In astrology, your sign is associated with the eighth house which is all about death, rebirth, transformation, and healing. Death is symbolic of change and when the Death card shows up it's just giving you a heads up. In the Death card you will see the image of a skeleton riding a white horse. The white horse represents hope and new life. In the distance you can see the sun rising again. This symbolism is similar to the life of a Scorpio. Even though you might struggle through dark times and cataclysmic changes you come out of it stronger and more resilient.

Life is all about change and as a Scorpio you are a natural when it comes to overcoming obstacles. You never give up! You are a fierce fighter and a survivor. Death is all about endings and also beginnings. Having to start over throughout your life is a common pattern for Scorpios. You will experience different cycles in your life where the person you were before is forever gone. Rising up and allowing change in your life helps you focus on the future. You are able to release and let go of old energy. This includes people who might not be good for you. Once you cut ties, then you don't look back. Your power comes from surrendering to the unknown and thriving on lasting change.

Element: Water

As a water sign, Scorpio is intuitive, emotional, and passionate. You have a powerful emotional nature that can sometimes be stormy. Out of all the water signs you are known to repress your feelings. Sometimes this is rooted in a desire to feel in control. If you avoid your feelings and repress them, then things can set you off. When you get angry it's a powerful force that impacts everyone around you. You are naturally self-protective and need solitude. Because of your ability to absorb other people's pain, you are often interested in helping others heal in some way. You are also good with managing other people's money and have skills in finance and business. Your emotions go through extremes because you don't feel things halfway. It's all or nothing for you in terms of your feelings. If you feel hurt you have the ability to cut people off quickly. This personality trait can actually help you guard your heart. But it can also make it hard to forgive others.

Personality Color: Blue

Scorpio is associated with the blue temperament. Blue personalities have depth and are intuitive. Commitment, loyalty, and trust are extremely important to you. There is a heightened intuition and psychic awareness that helps you connect deeply with other people. You need relationships and want to connect deeply with other people. There is a part of you that is introverted and protective, but deep down you are highly emotional and experience strong feelings. There is a powerful emotional ability that you possess. You also enjoy listening to other people's problems. Most of the time people that have pain are drawn into your life. You are a natural psychologist and counselor who enjoys offering practical, realistic, and transforming advice to those who ask. There is a deep desire to merge with another person and having intimacy in your life is key. You don't do well with lukewarm emotions because you prefer to experience intense passion. Having loyal and trustworthy friends, co-workers, and family will bring you joy.

The Scorpio Current Life Relationship Landscape

If you were born under the sign of Scorpio, your way of perceiving the world is lined with emotional intensity.

Your relationships are an important component on your road to self-discovery. You have a natural way of learning from real life experiences. The traditional astrology phrase for your sign is "I empower." Your belief in someone can motivate their self-confidence to pursue new goals. You do expect others to return their support for your own personal aspirations.

Relationships are a type of ritual in your belief system. You likely value loyalty and it is the cornerstone for you to trust those closest to you. You detest betrayal because it feels like a stab in the back. You prefer emotional honesty most of the time, although it must be said at times you are not ready to handle the truth. You prefer that lovers and friends be patient with your decision making. Some think you purposely take too long to make important decisions. You see this more as taking the time to carefully process the pros and cons involved. You like coming out as the winner in negotiations but don't always like revealing this.

Passion comes from the depths of your emotions. You border on possessing a partner but at the same time want those you love to exert their independence. Sharing power with your lovers wins their admiration. There are those fearing your blunt spoken words about them, but many find your direct communication refreshing.

You can be generous with your mental and physical resources. You know how to empower with your facial expressions as much as your actions. Then again, you will hold back your support for those who don't appreciate you. You like being cherished but might push back against being overly possessed by someone. You will open up your feelings if a person can be trusted. There are occasions when you need time to yourself as privacy is sacred to your mind and soul. You do like being held in the arms of a lover. Finding a soul mate feels like a safe world and one worth treasuring.

The Scorpio Past Life Karmic Relationship Patterns

You are not alone when it comes to bringing in past life patterns into the current incarnation. Our soul has traveled along a journey over several lifetimes. A repeating pattern of behavior from some of your past lives could have followed you into this life. These memories can become activated in various relationship encounters. If you find yourself identifying with any of the past life patterns discussed, don't see this as a judgment of yourself. In embarking on a path to gain clarity and new understanding about these shadowy energies you are taking steps to new self-discovery.

As a Scorpio, you have the mental and emotional strength to overcome any of the past life patterns. Your sense of personal power rises as you break loose from the hold of karmic patterns. It does require patience to stay determined to change a behavior into a more favorable light. Think of it as a learning experience to convert what was a pattern of behavior interfering with your relationship happiness into a positive expression. Enjoy the journey to greater knowledge.

Under My Thumb

When this past life pattern becomes activated, there is a tendency to fear not being in control. What is the result of this thinking? Usually, a Scorpio tendency is to want to overpower others. A territorial instinct needing to be preserved will release bossy tendencies. It impedes your growth in relationships to establish a genuine intimacy. It is possible you don't realize this shadow lodged in your past life memory is part of the way you handle yourself in relating to others. When challenged by someone, you may resist acknowledging that you embrace this pattern. The love and happiness you hope for becomes a distant reality if you don't shake the hold of this past life energy.

Another way this past life pattern can come into your life is through someone else conducting themselves in this way.

This is saying it might be a pattern you came into this life to overcome, and you are seeing it in another person. You are getting a front row seat to realize you don't want to go down this path. Sometimes we attract someone indulging in a past life energy we have come into the current life to conquer. It is critical to not come under the spell of that person.

Lost in Silence

Scorpio is a water sign which denotes deep emotional energy. There can be instincts to hide your feelings. This pattern surfaces when you are having a difficult time with trust. Those people closest to you may wonder what you are thinking when trying to get you to talk. You could be perceived as purposely retreating into a state of hibernation when it comes to sharing your true opinions. It is a fact that Scorpio individuals like yourself prefer to carefully process information. You may forget that others need you to come out of your reflection so that they can hear you verbalize your likes and dislikes. If you don't participate in enough communication, the intimacy you desire is not going to become a reality. Recharging your battery through taking some quiet time is normal. It is only when you use it as an excuse to hold back your feelings that this pattern intensifies and the love you need might lessen.

Angry Moods

This past life pattern has its roots deep in hidden anger. Anger is a raw emotion and if allowed to build with no release valve, eventually will explode. If you don't let out intense feelings they can interfere with your perceptions. Worse, your anger may be launched at someone over a situation quite unrelated to what you originally became upset over. Scorpio moods are a barometer about how you are feeling. They let you know how you are reacting to the behavior of others. It sometimes is better to let out your emotional intensity in the present. Another way this past life energy can manifest is if you have a regular habit of trying to push others to always agree with you through acting out angry moods. You don't then win the closeness you might hope to achieve. People will more than likely pull away when you display this pattern. An ocean of resentment from people is often the end result of falling into this shadowy energy.

Holding Grudges

Scorpio has an instinct to sometimes have trouble letting go of a person's past transgressions. They can be viewed as an absolute taboo. This past life pattern finds new life if you continue to dislike someone, even if they are no longer exhibiting the behavior that previously disturbed you. It can keep a relationship from growing if you let this pattern infiltrate your thinking. You don't have to forget how you don't like a person's past actions. But if you cannot forgive there may be a rift between you and someone close that is hard to fix. It is even possible that this shadowy energy might drain your mental energy. Staying too often locked in this pattern keeps you attached to a negative thought pattern, which in turn keeps you from the happiness you want to have in a relationship.

Extreme Jealousy

If you allow this pattern into your current incarnation, it drives a wedge between you and a person you care about. It can be a case of not trusting someone even if they give you no reason to feel this way. The underlying reason for this pattern is often fear of losing a lover or friend to someone else. It can be that you don't want to act like this but can't shake the influence of this shadowy force. It might be that camping out in your past life memories are images of being abandoned or betrayed. It does not mean that it will occur again in this life, but you are still being pulled back into those past memories. You lose your sense of personal empowerment if you keep giving into this past life pattern. Your own self-worth is getting lost in not feeling someone is truly valuing you. Your dependency needs become out of balance if you stay in this pattern of thinking.

There is another way this past life pattern can approach you. Someone you know may be directing this jealous behavior at you. It may surprise you that a lover could not trust you. The key thing here to remember is that you are being given an opportunity to perceive this pattern in someone else but don't need to walk down this path yourself.

Denial

This is a past life pattern that, if it becomes too present in your life, will find you denying what you perceive in a relationship thinking it will keep the peace. If this becomes an ongoing event, you could be missing out on getting your needs met. There is a little denial in all relationships, but if you are going way beyond your limits to remain in a relationship you are getting a bad deal. You are putting that Scorpio ability to do a reality check on the back burner, meaning you are only seeing what you want to see. Those insights you possess are getting too watered down, fogging your self-honesty. You could be enabling behaviors in not speaking truthfully to someone about how their words and actions are impacting you.

This pattern can come to you through a person in denial as to how they are treating you. It does not seem to matter how many times you speak up, the behavior continues. This could be a past life pattern you acted out yourself in previous incarnations. You have attracted an individual displaying this pattern firsthand. The universe is trying to show you this is a past life pattern you don't want to act out in your own life.

Over Analyzing

The Scorpio tendency to think through experiences deeply can go to the extreme, opening the door potentially to this past life pattern. You could be looking for what could go wrong in a relationship too much. Your sign is known for processing your thoughts carefully. There is a chance you might not give a relationship enough time to develop before giving up on it. The fear of adversity could be what is activating this pattern. Rather than work through a problem with someone, the temptation to escape starts occupying your thinking. You may be creating a crisis without realizing you are doing it. If you have a habit of leaving a relationship and not wanting to deal with your differences with a person, it may be linked to this pattern. In not trusting you can communicate more openly, it makes establishing a clear commitment difficult.

Too Much Pessimism

This past life pattern, when becoming too much of a reality, indicates lost hope in thinking you can find the right relationship. This could be due to disappointing experiences from past relationships in this life and very possibly those that occurred in past lives. As a Scorpio you will feel the pain of a relationship that has ended very deeply. Your normal ability to process your way through a disappointing love or friendship gets stuck in this pattern. The residue from a past life failed relationship might be compounding the problem in letting go of a current person. It is probably not so obvious that a past incarnation could be contributing to a delay in working your way through feelings you have for someone in this current life. Being too attached to a negative outlook might keep you from a relationship that promises harmony.

I Will Not Be Moved

It is natural for the Scorpio sign to defend its position on a decision. It is when you are not willing to consider any other options that this past life pattern can appear. Stubbornly standing your ground too much of the time eventually causes friction in a relationship. You may be dedicated to your own preferences to the point that reaching a compromise stays out of reach. The closeness you want with someone is difficult to have if you will not budge in your ideas as needed. That Scorpio instinct to want things on your own terms becomes a very dominant force if this pattern is too large an influence. It could be an underlying fear of not trusting others that keeps you holding hands with this shadowy force, and that prevents you from enjoying greater relationship fulfillment.

Twisting the Truth

If this pattern is too active in your life there is a tendency to tell people what they want to hear. It is a way to manipulate others into doing what you need them to do. Honest communication is missing. You have a hidden agenda that is in your own best interest. This is a type of passive aggressive pattern that in the end tends to backfire. It usually does not end up bringing the harmony you need with someone. This pattern is linked to hiding behind a persona you are displaying that only serves to cause confusion. Another theme running through this pattern is a fear of closeness. When this pattern is too active in your life, communication is intended to be a tool to keep others at a distance.

There is another way this past life pattern could appear in your life. Someone you know well may be in the habit of showing this behavior. It could seem eerily familiar and make you feel uncomfortable when you are aware of the pattern. It is your opportunity to recognize it and choose not to make use of it in your own life.

Power Struggles

There are occasions you need to defend your decisions. This past life pattern manifests when you go to extremes on a regular basis to prove you are right. The equal sharing of power, if missing in action, keeps the harmony in your relationships from being achieved. This pattern is often linked to a need to stay in control. If you trust someone enough to relinquish some of your power, it brings people closer. There is a strong, maintaining instinct in Scorpio. If an individual is perceived as disrupting your comfort zones, a desire to stand your ground emerges. A failure to openly communicate and be open to opposing viewpoints brings great tension into your relationships. The energy it takes to resist compromising can drain your energy. Defining your territorial needs too rigidly keeps love and intimacy at a distance.

Lack of Assertiveness

Self-doubt creeps into your life too much of the time when this past life pattern gains strength. This is the repeat of a pattern from past lives in letting others negate your thoughts. Your goals shut down and get taken over by the strong opinions of someone else. Your inner strength is there but held back by being too cautious. A fear of ridicule has you keeping your insights in the shadows. The faith to pursue your own dreams is missing. Being in the company of individuals with extreme self-interest will overshadow the footsteps you need to walk toward your own future goals. Living out the hopes and wishes of others stifles your own pursuits. Staying in limiting relationships keeps you from finding the love and acceptance in more fulfilling relationships.

The Scorpio Reward for Using Your Sixth Sense Intuitive Perception to Solve Karmic Patterns

When you release a karmic pattern, the world seems to open up new possibilities for happiness and self-discovery. Your mental energy will feel invigorated. Positive thoughts are more likely to fill the vacuum left when you let go of a past life pattern's influence. You may even find that intimacy and trust with others is easier to establish. The love you hope to experience can become a greater reality. Brave new perceptions can seem like a rebirth.

Don't be disturbed if one or more of the past life patterns discussed sounds like thoughts and actions you have acted out. Think of this as a learning experience. It is like a cosmic composting, taking negative energy and channeling it into more productive directions. Taking the first steps to confront a karmic pattern is the path to clearer insights. It can require practice and patience to get unentangled from a pattern from previous incarnations. Releasing the hold of this energy opens your mind to awakened ideas that can lead to relationship harmony. The confidence to overcome a past life pattern will come faster than you might have imagined.

The Under My Thumb pattern is less likely to occur if you stay away from controlling behaviors. It is natural for a Scorpio to have territorial needs. In letting those people you are closest to have their own sense of freedom, it empowers your relationships. When people know you trust them to make their own decisions, the communication flows more smoothly. Encouraging lovers and friends to exert their independence allows for intimacy to become a reality. This is a pattern that can hide from your conscious mind. Acknowledging this behavior brings it out from the shadows so you can begin to change.

There are occasions a past life pattern becomes visible through someone you know. Having the awareness to not adopt this pattern for yourself keeps it from resurfacing in your own behavior. Sometimes we attract individuals acting out a pattern we have come into this life to overcome. If you are in a relationship with a person displaying this pattern, be happy you recognize this is not a behavior you want for yourself.

The Lost in Silence pattern only needs you to communicate more openly. When you don't expect people to read your mind and you talk openly, it allows people to come closer.

Your emotions have a tendency to run deep. When you make a conscious effort to let someone into your inner world, the harmony you seek can happen. It may seem awkward at first if you are not good at expressing your ideas openly. With practice it gets easier. If you need some space, it is a good idea to tell someone. Privacy is highly valued by you being a Scorpio. You could be surprised that a loved one might not mind you taking time to yourself. The key is when you are in the company of those you love and appreciate, be sure to stay visible. Be an active listener as it does wonders for creating a bridge to a real shared, fulfilling relationship.

The Angry Moods pattern is less likely to surface again in this lifetime through expressing your feelings more openly. It is true that in some instances you may need to cool down before overreacting to someone else's words or actions. There is an emotional intensity linked to the passion you feel. But holding back anger for extended periods often enlarges an issue you have with someone. Having the trust that a person will not run away from you if you let out your true feelings comes with practice. Tuning into your moods can actually put you in touch with your clearest intuitive insights. You are likely sensitive to the energy of other people. Getting some meditative time to yourself is a great way to calm down moods and stay centered. Anger in itself is not a bad thing and can indicate you have feelings that must be communicated. When you don't fear your emotional power, it puts you closer to rising above this pattern and opens the door to relationship fulfillment.

The Holding Grudges pattern only needs you to redirect what has been a negative use of a powerful memory ability in a positive direction. Rather than holding on to energy that is working against you, there is a fast sense of relief when walking out of this past life pattern. It might take some conscious effort to move away from this pattern of thinking, but you will be glad you did. Your relationships will go smoother. The communication will have a flow that has a greater promise of mutual cooperation with someone. When you let go faster of negative perceptions of someone, the emotional closeness is easier to feel. Getting the support for your goals will be there when you need it. The less you sit in judgment of others, they will be likely to do the same for you. The road to harmony with others has fewer obstacles when breaking free from this pattern.

The Extreme Jealousy pattern frees you in many ways when you find the determination to let go of this tendency. When you establish your own unique sense of independence, this pattern disappears. Perceiving that jealousy only serves to take away from your personal power allows you a feeling of liberation. You will then attract the type of people who you can trust. Your path to fulfilling relationships gains clarity when you find the willpower to release jealous urges. The less you worry about what you could lose, the more it fills you with new insights. You gain a new wealth of energy by rising above this past life influence. Your dependency needs come into balance when you tap into your own self-worth. You enjoy your relationships more as you take the risk of trusting others and believing in your ability to pursue people who will be there when you need them.

If you happen to be in a relationship with a person caught in this pattern you need to use that Scorpio insight to be aware of it. This may have been a past life pattern you came here to overcome. Having the awareness to see this behavior in someone else is likely going to keep you from falling back into this past life influence.

The Denial pattern will be less of an issue if you admit to yourself that a behavior you dislike in someone must be faced. If you speak up and tell someone how their words and actions are impacting you, it is an empowering experience. You need to draw a line in the sand as to what you can tolerate. The road to having inner peace and finding harmony in a relationship is within your grasp when putting denial behind you. If this has been a pattern shadowing you for a long time, it takes some persistent determination to walk away from its influence. You will get more of what you need from others when moving beyond staying in denial only to keep someone happy with you. If you are in the right relationship, your lovers and friends will be able to handle how you really feel.

It is possible this pattern is being presented to you through an individual you know. A person is in a state of denial as to how they are interacting with you. Think of it as the universe giving you an opportunity to get a view of this pattern to allow you to realize you don't want to accept this as your own reality.

It is a good idea with the Over Analyzing pattern to have as a mantra that there are no perfect people. It will keep you from worrying too much about the things you don't like to the exclusion of the positives. The ability to research and have in-depth insights is a valuable trait for Scorpio to display. Being harder on the problems than on a person is a wise path to follow as well. Taking the time to get to know someone could allow you to see the potential of a solid relationship. Relationships can get messy at times. In not letting the first sign of adversity make you retreat from a relationship, you gain inner strength. You have a wonderful capacity to communicate with a lover or friend on a deep level based on trust. The reward for warming up to a commitment outweighs the fear of adversity. The intimacy and happiness you can enjoy with a trusted partner may make this past life pattern a faraway memory.

The Too Much Pessimism pattern needs you to get a brighter outlook in finding partners that share what you value in life. This pattern challenges you to stop judging people you meet based on what has happened in past relationships. What may not be so obvious are the painful, past life relationship memories residing in your subconscious mind. This might be keeping you from believing in the possibility of finding someone you can find harmony with in this life. Taking those first steps in trusting that you deserve relationship happiness opens the door for new possibilities. Survival instincts are strong in Scorpio. If you think positive it awakens a rebirth in you. This can be the key to attracting the right type of person. You might be surprised how fast you can turn the corner away from this past life influence with a new, vibrant attitude.

The I Will Not Be Moved past life pattern needs you to show some flexibility. People respond to you with less resistance when you are willing to adapt to change. Trusting that it is okay to not have to willfully hold on to your normal way of doing things brings people closer. When you are letting others feel they are being included in major decisions, it is the road to harmony. It may take some practice to change this pattern of behavior, but you will find the effort will pay off. Truly listening and being open to new ideas adds an empowering quality to your relationships. This might be a past life energy not so obvious to your conscious awareness. But you could be surprised that, with some regular effort, you will intuitively awaken and rise above this past life pattern.

The Twisting the Truth pattern can be less of a force in your life when you become a straight shooter in communicating with people. It can feel like a really scary leap of faith to trust someone. The interesting thing is that it takes less energy to be honest with others than continuously having a hidden agenda. Those first steps toward opening up in a truthful way may feel awkward at first. It is like developing a new habit in retraining your mind to not hide what you need from someone. Surrendering a tendency to manipulate when communicating allows for true intimacy and a closeness you can trust.

If this pattern is being presented to you through the actions of someone else, consider it an opportunity to realize you don't need to act it out yourself. This could be a past life energy that you came into this life to overcome. In seeing it in someone else, you can make a decision not to walk back into this past life influence.

The Power Struggles past life pattern is less likely to re-occur if you realize you don't need to always be right. This pattern becomes less of a reality if you share the wealth of your power. It may sound strange, but as you empower others it strengthens your own personal power. It takes much less energy out of you when you don't constantly force your ideas on others. Your passion for your own way of perceiving the world can inspire people to pursue their own goals. Being more of a team player is a path to creating harmony in your relationships. When you don't fear appearing vulnerable, people want to share their own inner world with you. Showing that you trust your intimate partners and friends wins their admiration. Allowing those you care about to chase after their own dreams ensures that this past life pattern will stay dormant.

The Lack of Assertiveness pattern has less impact in your life when you don't allow others to negate your insights. Taking the risk to promote your own goals pushes this past life pattern out of the way. It is true that as a water sign the emotions of Scorpio can sensitize you to the energy of others. It might take some practice, but eventually as you speak with conviction, people will listen. Trusting your own intuitive inner voice will help you rise up above individuals too critical of your opinions. The equality and harmony you want to find in relationships becomes a reality when you walk with self-confidence. When you step out of the shadows of someone else's self-serving dreams, you will discover like-minded souls who will support your own dreams.

The Scorpio Reward from Solving Karmic Patterns

It can be a surprise to realize a past life pattern has been active for quite some time in your life. Don't judge yourself. The effort you make in overcoming a past life influence pays great dividends. Your relationships will come into a clearer balance as you gain insight about any past life shadowy energy. As your understanding comes into the light, a past life pattern will be less bothersome. Scorpio has a great capacity to take energy that has been working negatively to a higher productive level. This can be experienced as a type of rebirth, giving a new vibrancy in how you relate to others.

You likely saw yourself in one or more of the past life patterns discussed. Remember they have no real control over you. With practice and patience, the self-discovery is exciting. You might even wonder why it took so long to convert a past life energy into creative and fulfilling outlets.

There may be occasions when you question whether you are making enough progress in dealing with a past life pattern. Think of it as a magical journey, allowing you energized mental and emotional vitality. Your eyes will open to a world with more options to participate in relationships with a promise of love and harmony.

Scorpio the Magician Journal Prompts

1. How do you feel when you see the Scorpio image?
2. What Scorpio archetype traits do you resonate most with?
3. Have you experienced loss or the death of someone close to you?
4. What healing abilities do you possess?
5. Do you have psychic and spiritual gifts?
6. Are you an all or nothing type of person?
7. What past life patterns have you experienced?

Chapter Nine

Sagittarius the Explorer

"I SEEK"
Keywords: Explorer, Adventurous, Optimistic, Friendly, Outgoing, Philosophical
Sun Sign Dates: November 21–December 20
Temperament: Choleric
Sign Type: Fire, Mutable
Planetary Ruler: Jupiter
Jungian Archetype: The Explorer
Tarot Card: Temperance
Polar Opposite Archetype: The Jester
Astrology Nickname: The Optimist
Polar Opposite Sign: Gemini
Symbol: The Archer
Personality Color: Orange, Extroverted
Rules: The Ninth House, The Thighs, Liver

Sagittarius Temperament: Choleric

Sagittarius is the ninth sign of the zodiac. Spontaneous at heart, you inspire others to believe in something bigger than themselves. You are known for your enthusiasm, strong opinions and need for action. Being straightforward and direct is your forte. You don't sugarcoat the truth but believe in being honest. The good news is you are able to give people direct feedback, delivered in a caring way. As a choleric personality you are a risk-taker and value your freedom. You are adaptable and seek excitement through exploration. As a high energy person, you can be indecisive and restless. Your impatience makes you blunt, but you also have an easygoing and adaptable personality. It is good for you to make time to relax and manage stress. It is good to take a break and ground your energy.

Jungian Archetype: The Explorer

Sagittarius is associated with the Explorer archetype. You are known to be adventurous and enjoy exploring new ideas, places, and connecting with new people. Travel to faraway, foreign lands or having the opportunity to live in another country might be very appealing. Sagittarius rules the ninth house in astrology which is an area of life where you pursue knowledge and wisdom. You can be a forever-student and enjoy studying religion, philosophy, law, and different languages. Connecting to people with similar belief systems and those who are different from you can be inspiring. You are a self-reliant and need freedom of movement in your life whether physically, mentally, or emotionally. Just like the Explorer archetype you are wise and seek deeper meaning in life. You can be a risk-taker and fiercely independent. It is important that you feel free in your relationships. You might choose to remain single or marry at an older age.

Being outdoors and having room to roam is key to your physical health. There is an inborn faith and optimism that helps you see the positive side of life. You attract blessings because of your ability to encourage others to be grateful for what they have. Learning about other people's cultures, beliefs, and customs helps you feel inspired. As a forever-student, you are always pushing yourself to learn something new and to seek truth wherever you go.

Tarot Card Archetype: Temperance

The esoteric symbol for fire is a triangle with the point upwards. Sagittarius is a fire sign, and you can see the triangle image on the angel's dress in this card. You are wise, seek the truth and like to learn new things. Your passion for seeking knowledge can be seen in this card as well. On the forehead of the angel is a circle, near the third eye chakra, representing clear sight. Just like the angel in the Temperance card with one foot on land and one in water, you are always connected to truth and don't allow emotions to get the best of you. As a Sagittarius, you enjoy travel, adventure, and exploring faraway places. The passion to travel and a forever wanderlust is symbolized in this card. In the distance you can see the path leading to the mountains and the image of the sun is shining there in the distance. The sun is symbolic of hope, happiness, and positivity which are all personality traits you possess. It also is symbolic of your optimistic and positive outlook.

Sign Element: Fire

Sagittarius enjoys being on the go! Constant movement and a restless energy push you forward to seek new experiences. Being a fire sign gives you energy to keep physically active. You don't like to be cooped up indoors for too long. Fresh air and being out in nature can bring peace and healing. Socializing, networking, and connecting to many different types of people inspires you. Bold, passionate, and friendly you like to flirt with others. But once someone shows an interest in more than friendship you might roam off into the distance. Fiercely independent and self-reliant, you don't want to feel possessed. Feeling free to pick up and change and do something in a moment's notice without having to worry about other people is appealing to you. You don't want to hurt other people's feelings, so sometimes you prefer to stay single. This helps you pursue your hobby of travel, adventure, and change.

Personality Color: Orange

Sagittarius is fun-loving, open-minded, passionate, and friendly. You share similar personality traits to the orange personality. Being able to feel autonomy and make decisions in the moment suits you best. Feeling controlled, trapped, or micro-managed will set off your alarm bells. You will rebel against authority if you feel you are not trusted to work freely. You are a high energy person who can get a lot done, but you aren't always good at planning. Inspiration comes in the moment and is a natural intuitive process. Making lists and checking them off is not your style. You get along well with other oranges which are the other fire signs, Aries and Leo. There will be a natural trust with green personalities, which are the air signs. Libras, Aquarians, and Geminis will pique your interest and you will communicate easily with them. You like adventure, excitement, and want to feel alive. Boring topics and mundane activities zap your spirit. You will excel due to an optimistic, positive, and happy-go-lucky attitude. Abundance and good luck comes your way because of your ability to adapt.

The Sagittarius Current Life Relationship Landscape

If you were born under the sign of Sagittarius, your insatiable optimism makes you very likeable. There is an urgency in you at times to share your thoughts with others. Gaining knowledge must be included in your regular mental diet. People who are bold in expressing their viewpoints get your attention. Closed-minded individuals might annoy you. Your lovers and friends like your expansive search for adventure and various kinds of new experiences. A traditional astrology slogan for Sagittarius is "I explore."

You are proud of your individualism and appreciate those who recognize this in you. Your idealism is passionate and inspiring. You thrive on having a like-minded partner and yet want to encourage independence. You like being depended on for advice but grow weary of people who lean too heavily on you.

Boredom is likely what you detest the most. You enjoy someone who challenges your ideas without judging you. Traveling with a lover on the mental and physical planes keeps life interesting. You might suddenly surprise someone with a new plan. If you give some advance notice of your desire for change it stabilizes your relationships.

Patience is sometimes challenging as you do have a restless spirit. You need multiple outlets for a creative mind. People probably perceive you as always being on the move, but you see this as a normal way to function in the world. When you take time to pause it allows others to keep up with you and catch their breath.

Your loyalty wins the hearts of those you love. There is a sincere, caring look in your eyes that individuals closest to you cherish. When you move forward to pursue goals and don't lose sight of your loved ones, harmony surrounds your relationships.

The Sagittarius Past Life Karmic Relationship Patterns

Everyone has some past life memories they brought into this incarnation. You probably will identify with one or more of the past life patterns that will be discussed. Don't let this worry you. Each of us has come into this life with lessons to learn. Think of it as an adventurous journey to self-discovery. It helps to keep patience in mind as you read about the past life patterns associated with your sign. If one of these past life influences has been active in several past lives, it takes practice to express the energy in a positive direction. Becoming aware of a past life pattern allows you to take steps to gain a new understanding.

As a Sagittarius, your desire to seek stimulating insights can guide you to overcome any past life influences. You have a never-ending optimism that is your key to responding to challenges. There is an inner quest in you to find a soul mate and supportive friends. It is these people-connections that give you the confidence to rise above a karmic pattern. The drive to find new routes to gain greater knowledge gives you the vision to navigate through any past life influences.

Too Judgmental

Sagittarius is known for being open to input from other people. If this past life pattern becomes awakened, your tendency to be close-minded can intensify. When you fight for an idea in a dogmatic way you alienate the individuals you are trying to win to your side. It is refusing to listen to opposing points of view that creates tension in your relationships. If you become too much of a critic, it causes others to distance themselves from you. It is okay to fight for your ideals. Where the problem comes into being is when you lose your objectivity. That tolerance to let people express themselves freely is missing. A rigid and inflexible attitude interferes with the harmony you want in how you relate to others.

Grass is Greener Elsewhere

This past life pattern has its roots in running away from a current relationship thinking there is a more perfect one waiting somewhere else. This can cause you to leave a promising relationship too early before it has had a chance to develop. Sagittarius is a fire sign and, occasionally, that impatience for situations to develop quickly is not realistic. The future seems more exciting than dealing with solving the everyday problems that can exist in even the best of relationships. Running away from what is believed to be too messy to search for that perfect partner is what is at the heart of this pattern. This past life influence is like a revolving door that will keep you suddenly jumping out of relationships. It will keep you on the run until you face that this past life pattern is taking you away from the fulfillment you hope to achieve with someone.

Hidden Emotions

At first glance you may appear easygoing and not difficult to get to know. If this past life influence grows too dominant, your emotions may be a challenge to express. It might feel like someone has to pry open where your inner world resides. A fear of revealing your emotions is what is holding you back. You may find it easy to talk about a wide variety of subjects. Staying on the mental level is your natural comfort zone. The trust a partner wants to have for you could be difficult if they sense you are holding back your feeling side. Not wanting to appear vulnerable is likely at the root of this pattern. It may be hurtful feelings left over from previous relationships in this life or previous incarnations that keep you stuck in this pattern of behavior. This is a shadowy energy that can keep the love from flowing between you and someone you care about.

Commitment Confusion

Sagittarius has an inner gypsy and travel urge. You might say these two traits keep you energized and enthusiastic about life. This pattern comes alive if you take the freedom principle too far. In other words, if this past life influence grabs you with too strong a grip, you may be an unpredictable free spirit. Someone wanting more of a clear commitment from you might seem unreasonable. Your idea of a commitment may be to come and go as you please. If you are wanting to keep someone close they might have trouble accepting your understanding of a commitment. Being depended on for emotional support makes you nervous when this pattern is a dominant force.

Another way this past life pattern might appear is if someone you are involved with is displaying it. You may have a hard time knowing if you can count on this person when you need them. Consider this an opportunity to get a close-up view of this as a pattern you don't want to express yourself. It could be a past life pattern you came into this life from which to escape.

Not Agreeing to Disagree

This pattern, when activated, finds you fighting for your own ideas to the exclusion of truly listening to those of others. When you lose perspective in considering any other options bar your own way of thinking, it creates distance with people. Your communication tries to drown out the words of those trying to engage with you in sharing ideas. This past life pattern influences you to take one-sided views of situations. It can keep arguments on fire with no resolutions in sight. Compromise is difficult to reach. Instead of love and intimacy with a partner you can end up with a broken heart. Sagittarius gives you a mental insight that can think a few moves ahead, like on a chess board. You have to ask yourself what it is worth to always play to win only what is best for you. This isn't the way to bring harmony into relationships.

Too Unpredictable

Your sign is one with a spontaneous mind that at times loves the thrill of new adventures. If this past life pattern manifests in full force it can disrupt the close connection you have with someone. You might quickly surprise someone on a regular basis with wanting to make a major change of direction. If you are never giving much advance notice about changing your mind, a lover may feel left out of your future plans. You may appear to be too difficult to be counted on when someone needs you. This may be a pattern residing in your memory bank from lives when you were a free spirit, moving with no desire for roots. It could be you are still replaying these memories. Your lovers and friends may perceive you as too self-centered, while you think of this as living out your dreams. It can be a big challenge to have any stability with someone if you forget to let them in on your life script. It is that sudden urge to live on impulse that may mean that those close to you find it difficult to stay along for the ride.

Denying Issues

Hearing only what you want to hear can bring this past life pattern into your everyday life. Issues that could be resolved quickly with honest communication get bigger when the discussion gets postponed to a later date. The optimism of Sagittarius can be used to act like there is nothing wrong in a relationship but in reality a problem is driving a wedge between you and someone else. The happy face you are wearing is trying to cover up dealing with adversity. Rather than work toward a solution there is a tendency in this pattern to hold back how you are really feeling. The mystery of trying to figure out how you are sizing up a situation can cause unclear communication. The fear of causing an argument is often worse than directly dealing with a situation as it presents itself. The natural spontaneity of Sagittarius is getting blocked by being too much in denial about negotiating clearly.

Fixation on Limitation

It seems like quite a contradiction for an optimistic Sagittarius to have a life dominated by lost hope. If this past life pattern has too big a say, it is difficult to see the cup at least half full. You may think because you have run into some bad luck regarding relationships that you can't get things turned around in your favor. It is very possible that embedded in your mind are memories that can be traced back to past incarnations when you ran into some relationship disappointments. The problem is that if this past life pattern gets activated, you could be stuck too much in negative memories about relationships from lives in past incarnations, rather than having a positive outlook about the current life. Focusing more on what is good in your life is being crowded out by what, in your mind, has gone wrong. The negative attitude is blocking the entrance of new people into your life.

Very High Expectations

Your belief in someone can bring out their best. But if you regularly have unrealistic expectations of them, it can be a sign this past life pattern has emerged. There is a natural optimism in Sagittarius that can work greatly for your own life. If superimposed on someone else, it might be too far out in front of their reality. It starts to feel to others that you are being too pushy in what you think is right for them. This can result in resentment and a tension that alienates those you are trying to help. Your enthusiasm that is meant to encourage can be pushing someone away. Your idealistic belief in a person can become too much of a mission that invades the space of someone you care about.

It is possible that someone close to you is embodying this pattern. They may have good intentions but are not aware of their over-encouragement of you in a direction you don't want to go. Even when you try to talk to them about their behavior it continues. Think of it as an opportunity to not accept this pattern for your own life. This could be a past life pattern you came into this life to overcome, and the universe is letting you perceive it in someone else.

My Way Is the Only Way

Sagittarius is known for having an openness to a wide variety of ideas. Where this past life pattern comes into play is if you expect your own ideas to always rule the day. This does cause a lover to keep you at arms-length much of the time. Usually, the source of this pattern is the need to stay in control of the dialogue. A lack of trust can be another contributing factor that keeps this past life shadow from coming out into the light. The tolerant quality found in Sagittarius is missing that allows you to consider the ideas of others with a mutual acceptance. This way of operating in the world makes the odds to find harmony in relationships less likely.

Self-Serving Goals

If this pattern becomes activated in this life, a great me-focus can grow very strong. You will lose sight of what others need from you. Your own goals come first too much of the time. You may expect support for your own future plans but are not paying attention to those of someone close to you. A compulsive drive for attention will begin to make people pull away. Sometimes it can be a cause a Sagittarius is dedicated to that might mean you expect a loved one to always put their own plans on hold. When you lose your perspective, only focusing on your own needs, it throws your relationships out of balance. The mutual respect for each other's ideas is missing.

Making Too Many Promises

Your sign sometimes bites off more than it can chew when it comes to making promises. This past life pattern may not be so obvious in your mind if you have this tendency. The driving force behind this pattern is wanting to please others. The problem comes when you have made promises and exaggerated your potential to fulfill them. The disappointment resulting from making unrealistic pledges serves to get people upset with you. This pattern could be traced back to past lives where you had a fear of not wanting to lose a lover. In trying to do too much, it made any issues between you and someone else bigger. This may be a type of pattern caused by avoiding honest communication about a problem with someone. To make the issue go away, you promise more than you can deliver, hoping it will make things better, but in reality it only delays really working out the disagreement.

The Sagittarius Reward for Using Your Sixth Sense Intuitive Perception to Solve Karmic Patterns

There is a renewed revitalization of mental and physical energy when letting go of the hold of a past life pattern. It can feel like your way of relating to others has gained new insights. You could even find yourself redefining what you need in a relationship. Your sense of empowerment is often enhanced through gaining clarity about past life patterns. There is a possibility your insights about people will climb to a higher altitude. There is a journey of self-discovery stimulated when responding to the challenge of balancing past life energies.

Don't get disturbed if one or more of the past life patterns discussed seem like part of your current life reality. Each of us has brought in past life memories. The key thing to remember is that it takes patience to work through a past life pattern. The first step is to awaken to the realization a pattern from your past life history may still be with you. You can then begin to find ways to not let it interfere with the harmony you hope to achieve. You have the capability to overcome any of the past life patterns.

The Too Judgmental pattern only needs your sharp ability to see the flaws in someone's thinking to exercise patience. Letting someone speak without interrupting their flow of reasoning is more apt to get them to hear your own logic. That Sagittarius ability to allow for more than one right answer to a subject of interest wins you greater cooperation. You are known as the student and the teacher of the zodiac signs. You stand a better chance to gain the knowledge from others when keeping an open mind. Rather than criticizing someone's opinions too strongly, let your mind stay objective. Giving others the freedom to speak even if you don't agree with them is a faster road to harmony. Acknowledging a lover or friend's insights is a sure way to get them to accept your point of view.

The Grass is Greener Elsewhere pattern is asking you to slow down and let a relationship have enough time to develop. There is an inner restlessness in all fire signs like Sagittarius. The spirit of adventure in your sign only needs to be channeled clearly. It is possible, in some past lives linked to this incarnation, that you were not comfortable in a long-term relationship or there were circumstances that prevented this from occurring. In the current life this memory might still be with you. There is a better chance you will find a deeper sense of fulfillment if you give a relationship long enough to reveal its true depth. This past life influence will lessen in intensity as you trust yourself enough to form a commitment in a relationship. Freedom is important to a Sagittarius. If you are in the right relationship, chances are your partner will value their own independence. When you get over fearing a stable relationship, you are most of the way there in rising above this pattern from past lives.

The Hidden Emotions pattern is easier to resolve when you get over a fear of letting someone know you on an emotional level. You may not even know on a conscious level that your intellect is glossing over your emotional nature. Opening up to this awareness is the first steps to overcoming this past life influence. Conversing about many different topics is always at your fingertips. You like to know what people are thinking. Sagittarians can become quite emotional when expressing their idealism and love for a cause. When you show your most intimate partners your feelings, they trust you in a big way. Fire signs like yourself sometimes project strength in not wanting to appear vulnerable. You may be surprised that many will find you even stronger when you let them into your feeling world.

The Commitment Confusion past life pattern plays off of your drive for wanting plenty of space to be yourself. If you are clear in respecting a partner's need to have the room to explore their own goals, you are well on your way to keeping this pattern from emerging. Making sure you are truly listening to what those closest to you need from you helps keep balance in your relationships. Often people just want to know that you are hearing their voice. If you act like a team player, your lovers and friends stay happier. It might be you pull away when someone wants a more defined commitment. Getting past a fear of closeness is the key to loosening the hold of this pattern.

There is a possibility you have met this past life pattern through someone else expressing it. This actually may be a past pattern from some of your other lives that you came here to transcend. Think of it as an opportunity to get a viewing of this pattern but a chance to not accept it as part of your own reality.

The Not Agreeing to Disagree pattern becomes less likely to make an appearance in your life when you think in terms of what is best for you and someone else. There is nothing wrong with fighting for your beliefs. Just be sure to think in terms of fairly considering the opinions of others. You will find you can persuade others to your way of thinking when letting them talk freely. There is a spontaneous emotional intensity in Sagittarius that can have an appeal. Your ideas are more readily accepted when you show you are willing to listen to alternative points of view. Your sign attracts support for your way of thinking when you keep the talk flowing in both directions. Staying aware of the impact of your words allows you to maintain a broad, tolerant objectivity.

The Too Unpredictable pattern does not have to come between you and those you love or want to maintain a relationship with in this life. Being born as a Sagittarius does give you an inner restlessness, that at times will find you wanting to make changes quickly. If you can give some advance warning there is a better chance someone will be more open to the new plan. If you keep your mind occupied with enough mental stimulation it could settle down impulses that disrupt your relationships. There is a need for a Sagittarius to have their eyes on being there for someone in the present as much as on future goals. Balancing an intensity to move fast with being patient with others is a key theme to keeping this past life influence away from you.

The Denying Issues pattern requires a change in how you approach problems that arise in a relationship. Taking those first steps to not hold back when you need to speak up about a disagreement may take some practice. There will come a time when your response time gets faster. This past life influence has less of a chance to manifest when you are more direct in communicating your thoughts. Much is gained when you offer your input and exchange ideas in a mutually beneficial way. Your thoughts on a subject often have a broad perspective that proves valuable. Finding that inner Sagittarius confidence to let your thoughts be visible may be met with a positive reaction that surprises you. This past life pattern is linked to how much you feel comfortable with sharing your insights. There are going to be tense situations in any relationship. There are times anger releases emotions that clear the air between people. The main thing to remember is that honest communication is more likely to get you closer to harmony.

The Fixation on Limitation pattern needs a refocusing of negative thinking into a new positive framework. The universe has a way of opening up new opportunities when you make room for them with a refreshed outlook. You don't need to settle for past memories whether from this life or previous incarnations. There is a river of optimism always flowing within a Sagittarius like yourself. It only takes more concentration on what could go right rather than on what can go wrong to bring new people into your life. There is luck in your sign that gets stronger when you believe in yourself. There is a magical synchronicity which means meaningful coincidences when you believe in abundance. You can cross over faster than you might think into a richer life surrounded by supportive people. It only takes those first few steps to keep a gratitude list in your mind. The universe will meet you halfway when you walk along a path of a positive energy.

The Very High Expectations pattern needs you to keep in mind that people you are close to have to go at their own pace. Your dreams may not be their own. Their imperfections don't need you to try to fix them anymore than you would want them to try to do this for you. It is great to encourage and inspire others. Be reasonable in what you expect, and this past life pattern does not become an issue. Your idealism at times becomes strong and you will want to lift others up. Just be sure you reality check to make sure you don't go too far beyond your own boundaries, especially if someone is not asking you to do so. Letting someone know you are there for them as needed is a wise path to ensure balance in your relationships.

If it is true an individual is too demanding of you based on their own expectations you will need to push back and let them know. It could be you are getting a glimpse of this pattern that you came into this life to overcome. It is your chance to gain the understanding that this is a past life influence that you don't want to put into your self-expression.

The My Way Is the Only Way pattern is a closed way of perceiving the ideas of others that needs a more expansive view. Your relationship with others gets a wonderful boost of energy when you stay away from dogmatic viewpoints. You attract the people that want to create harmony with you when you stay flexible. Surrendering controlling behaviors keeps those you love close. It is easier to rise above the issues that face you and those you love when listening with an open mind. Your sign has a built-in capacity to accept people the way they are rather than pushing for your own agenda. The fulfilling relationships you can enjoy come to you when making a concerted effort to listen to alternative insights. It is the sure way to keep this past life influence a distant stranger.

The Self-Serving Goals pattern only needs your passion for what is important to you, not to lose sight of what the main people in your life value for their own future. It is wonderful to pursue your own passionate interests. Encouraging your lovers and friends to go after their own dreams wins their admiration. Having some shared projects goes far in empowering your relationships. That Sagittarius enthusiasm when offered to others is highly appreciated. Your belief in someone gets them to want to support your own goals. Sharing your knowledge with individuals has a way of bringing great companions along your life journey.

The Making Too Many Promises pattern needs you to be reasonable in what you can do for others to make them happy. It keeps your relationships in balance when the give and take is equal. There is the possibility for over confidence in believing you can do the impossible for someone. Having a reality check before trying to please someone is wise. Rather than not dealing with an issue with a person, you might be surprised to find it easier to talk over a problem. The direct approach takes less energy than making unrealistic promises. Chances are that intimacy and harmony is easier to achieve when having the confidence to work through a problem. Keeping that Sagittarius' desire to make someone happy to a reasonable level is the path to keeping this past life tendency in check.

The Sagittarius Reward from Solving Karmic Patterns

The world would be missing a bright-eyed, optimistic influence without the sign Sagittarius. Your ability to see the cup at least half full gives you the edge in overcoming any past life pattern. It does take your fiery, feisty energy to not lose confidence in taking those first steps to navigate through a pattern's influence. Patience is important because some past life memories have a tendency to hang on to us longer. You can outlast these past life energies and win them over into a positive expression.

If one or more of the past life patterns discussed sound like they are part of your self-expression, don't let it worry you. Each of us has past life shadow forces we are trying to gain clarity about. Be glad you are awakening to a new possible way of expressing these energies and thought patterns.

A fire sign like Sagittarius can get in a hurry to solve a problem. Try to remember that overcoming a past life pattern takes time. The more you gain greater awareness about a pattern, the more its influence lessens. The persistent effort to seek self-growth will guide you to the relationship harmony and joy you hope to discover.

Sagittarius the Explorer Journal Prompts

1. How do you feel when you see the Sagittarius image?
2. What Sagittarius archetype traits do you resonate most with?
3. Where would you like to travel?
4. What do you like to study and learn?
5. Do you have interest in different philosophies?
6. Are you a free spirit?
7. What past life patterns have you experienced?

Chapter Ten

Capricorn the Ruler

"I Use"

Keywords: Conservative, Ambitious, Responsible, Hardworking, Disciplined, Cautious

Sun Sign Dates: December 21–January 19

Temperament: Melancholic

Sign Type: Earth, Cardinal

Planetary Ruler: Saturn

Jungian Archetype: The Ruler

Tarot Card: The Devil

Polar Opposite Archetype: The Caregiver

Astrology Nickname: The Achiever

Polar Opposite Sign: Cancer

Symbol: The Goat

Personality Color: Gold, Introverted

Rules: The Tenth House, Knees and Joints

Capricorn Temperament: Melancholic

Capricorn is the tenth sign of the zodiac. You are super responsible and mature for your age and can feel different than your friends. You take things seriously and sometimes feel uncomfortable showing your feelings. Other people might perceive you as rigid and emotionally distant, but this is just a defense mechanism. You are loyal and protective of people you care about. You are a realist and see the world in a practical way. There is a tendency for you to doubt yourself and be pessimistic. Disciplined and determined, you work hard for what you want. You are prone to struggle with dark moods and periods of depression. You need time alone to dwell and process your feelings to feel better. After you brood for a while you snap out of it and are back out trying to accomplish your goals.

You have a melancholic personality and this makes you introverted. There is a strong connection to family and tradition. Working hard and being disciplined come naturally. Cautious and goal-oriented, you can be successful at work because of your long-term planning skills. Being committed and productive helps you attract opportunities for advancement. You seem to connect with the right people who can help open doors for you at work. You need to respect someone in order to want them in your life. Making friends with people who can benefit your life happens naturally.

Jungian Archetype: The Ruler

Capricorn is associated with the Ruler archetype and rules the tenth house in astrology. The tenth house is all about career, recognition, success, leadership, and having a public image. Similar to the Ruler energy you are traditional and like systems that are structured. As the Ruler archetype, you are a natural leader and want to be in charge. You might find it difficult to work for other people. There is a sense of drive, responsibility, and authority that seem to play out in your life in many different ways. Sometimes you have to be careful of being a tyrant or becoming too rigid. As a Capricorn, the dark side of your personality resists showing vulnerability and you can be too hard on yourself. As the goat in astrology, you work hard to climb up the mountain. You never give up. In the end you want to reach the top of the mountain. Destined to be a ruler once you obtain wisdom, you will find yourself moving up the ladder. You are meant to lead others in some way and with experience you learn important lessons to help you understand others. Be patient and understand that time and patience bring you good luck.

Tarot Card Archetype: The Devil

Capricorn is associated with father energy. Saturn brings a sense of responsibility and karmic lessons that need to be overcome. The Devil card is symbolic of Capricorn's hidden personality. This energy can enhance your desire for materialism, money, and deep down you like to have control. Every sign has positive and negative traits that need to be balanced. You are sometimes known to be hard, strict, and conservative in your views. There is a need for discipline and structure. It can be difficult for you to relax. It's hard for you to be carefree and easygoing. You may resist being vulnerable or showing others how you really feel. You are connected to power and possess intense ambition. Making a lot of money sometimes equals success in your mind. With age you realize that money doesn't always bring happiness. The Devil card reminds you to be careful about focusing too much of your energy on things in the outside world. Balancing work, and ambition with spending time with people you care about can make things easier in your relationships. You want to provide materially for your family, but your loved ones also need quality time with you.

The Devil card symbolism is a warning about not focusing too much on selfish desires and getting stuck in heavy materialism. Happiness does not always come from having money, possessions, or physical pleasures. You are here to learn this important lesson. You need to be patient with yourself and resist the karma of feeling chained to the darker side of life. It will be helpful to work on releasing your controlling behaviors. Capricorn and the Devil archetype both learn liberation through balancing practical goals with feelings and emotions.

Sign Type: Earth

Capricorn embodies all the traits of an earth sign. You are grounded, patient, and reliable. You are practical, realistic, and hardworking which pushes you hard to achieve your goals.

Born with a calculating mind, you are always thinking about ways you can accumulate wealth. Feeling safe and secure in the real world helps you maintain a sense of comfort. You like to control things and realize that you can work hard in the material world to accumulate what you want. Planning and dedicating your time to tasks helps you feel productive. There are very few people who can work as hard or as long hours as you can. Your sign is associated with the tenth house of success and career.

As an earth sign, you value stability and financial independence. It is important for you to have commitment in relationships. You can be attracted to tradition and success. As the achiever of the zodiac, you are determined to make enough money to buy the things you want. You also take family responsibilities seriously and want to help support their needs. Because you are traditional and conservative in your views you have high standards. Sometimes rigid and unforgiving, you have to realize that everyone is not as dedicated as you.

Personality Color: Gold

Capricorn is structured and wants things to be organized. Being an earth sign makes you a classic gold personality. Golds need a schedule and want stability in life. You need stability and order in your environment. Sometimes you feel a sense of duty and responsibility to work harder than other people. You like to take charge of situations and create a productive approach. Getting tasks completed in a timely manner brings you happiness. You also like to be the one telling other people what to do. If you are not in charge, you need to respect and look up to those who you work for. You will have a hard time letting go of your need to control things. Where you can get into conflict is when you try to control how others do things. Not everyone will do things like you do, so you have to learn to be less rigid about your expectations. You are a rule follower and respect traditions, hierarchy, and believe in building your success slowly. One of the most patient signs, you are dedicated when you commit to something. You are reliable and people can count on you. At work, you will work well with other gold personalities which are also earth signs, such as Taurus and Virgo. Clashes in relationships can occur with orange and green personalities. They want to do things differently and like to buck authority, which makes you uncomfortable.

Capricorn Current Life Relationship Landscape

If you were born under the sign Capricorn you are attracted to individuals with a sound logic. Those who show they understand your serious goals are appreciated. The traditional phrase in astrology for Capricorn is "I build." You are a steady planner and believe in finishing what you begin. You take commitments seriously and like people who honor them. You are more hard working than many people you encounter. Ambition likely came early in life. You attract responsibility because you appear trustworthy and responsible.

When you trust someone, you expect this in return. There can be a cautiousness in beginning love or friendship types of relationships. Some people may perceive you as being emotionally reserved. You likely see this as wanting to make sure someone is worth revealing yourself to. You can be depended upon during a crisis which is admirable. There is an inner strength that manifests during adversity that may even surprise yourself.

People with business sense are appreciated. You like grounded people with clearly defined goals. Then again being surprised by those you love can warm your heart. You have an ability to focus on a goal that is the envy of the other astrological signs. There is a possibility a special person in your life would be encouraging you to be more flexible.

Sharing your wisdom with others brings them closer. If you don't try to be too controlling the intimacy and harmony you hope for are within your grasp. When you show unconditional love, romance and friendship come to greet you.

Your persona might display a serious face. When you let down your guard it invites people to get to know you on a deeper level. You have a tendency to test the reality of your goals. In many ways you believe in trust, but verify it. Your relationships flow better when you are at ease with your life journey. Having a soul mate to celebrate anniversaries and special milestones with makes taking a chance on someone worth every bit of the effort.

Capricorn Past Life Karmic Relationship Patterns

There is no need to be anxious if you identify with any of the past life patterns that will be discussed here. Everyone has brought in past life material to work on. Keep a positive attitude. Any past life energy takes some practice to gain greater awareness in understanding it. You gain empowerment in channeling a past life pattern into a productive expression. Taking those first steps in bringing past life influences out of the darkness and into the light for clearer insight is the path to self-discovery.

As a Capricorn you have that steady, disciplined approach to life pursuits. You can take that sure-footedness to solve a past life pattern and open the door to more fulfilling relationships. It is not uncommon to wonder if you are making progress in rising above a past life shadowy energy. If you keep your mind away from over-analyzing, you will find the journey of tuning into a clear vision to make peace with a past life pattern, that much more pleasurable.

I am the Boss

This pattern is one in which you are leaving out opinions from others due to exclusive loyalty to your own. This is a tendency that might be hidden deep in your memory and not so obvious to your conscious awareness. The impact of this pattern is that closeness in relationships is difficult to establish. A failure to listen to others' viewpoints can isolate you from receiving information that might be helpful to consider. The underlying source of this pattern is often an inability to trust. It is a turnoff when someone realizes you don't hear their voice on important decisions affecting you both. That shared feeling of mutual respect is missing.

Rigid Focus

If this pattern gains too much influence, it is a product of your great focusing power on ideas but lacking flexibility. This type of thinking has a tendency to alienate individuals you are trying to bring closer. Intimacy and love get blurred if you hold onto this past life shadow. Commitments are harder to keep strong with lovers and friends if they regularly perceive you as unwilling to ever compromise. Your dedication to a cause may be a good thing but it can cause problems if you forget to support the needs of those who care about you. If you stay too protective of your own insights and block out those of others, it causes great tension in your relationships.

On My Guard

Capricorns can be very hesitant about revealing emotions to others. It can feel like you are losing your sense of personal power if you show your feelings. If this becomes a way of thinking that grows too extreme, it is a sign that this past life pattern has become activated. In being too guarded, there appears to be a wall between you and another when they try to read your inner world. Your communication is more comfortable on a business level but stalls on the emotional highway. You could be expecting others to guess what is on your mind rather than communicating openly. The rings in the sky that surround your ruling planet, Saturn, are similarly guarding those feelings that come from the heart.

Conditional Love

There is a strategy side of Capricorn that serves you well in negotiations that can be of great benefit to you and others. Where this past life pattern could make an appearance is if you are not going to express love for someone without any conditions. You may be over structuring how you give affection to someone, without getting what you need from them first. This does not create the closeness and harmony you hope to have. There is a lack of letting things flow between you and those you love. People need you to be less agenda-motivated and more spontaneous in sharing love. The more you make rules to guide your outpouring of love toward someone, the less likely you are going to find the fulfillment you seek in relationships.

Addicted to Negative Thinking

When your mind is working in the right direction and playing off positive energy, there is nothing you can't accomplish. If this past life pattern gets kick-started, your negative thinking becomes too much in charge of the way you see the world. This can interfere with how you perceive the actions of others in a too judgmental way. Your words then have a tendency to arouse anger rather than harmony when trying to make joint decisions. It is very possible you are looking for too much perfection in others. Love and fulfillment are not easy to have with a lover or friend if you accent the negative and set impossible standards.

This is one of those past life energies that could come into your life through someone close to you. There is a chance you came into this incarnation to make peace with this pattern of behavior. The key thing to remember is not to get hooked into this past life shadow yourself. The universe is giving you an opportunity to recognize this pattern in someone else and not make it part of your own reality.

Weak Assertiveness

An indication this past life pattern has become activated is if your assertiveness in relating to others freezes up too much of the time. It is true a trait of Capricorn is wanting to carefully make sure an idea will be a success before making it visible to others. In relationships you could become frustrated if it seems like your goals are not valued. You may be overly attached to a past life memory where not getting your needs met was a regular event. This may be how this energy finds an opening into the current incarnation. The patience and reserved tendencies in an earth sign like Capricorn can be taken advantage of by others when your assertiveness is registering too low. Eventually this might turn into hidden anger if you allow someone to keep pushing your goals backward rather than forward.

Too Austere

Your expectations of people become too strict if this past life pattern becomes too prevalent a force in your life. Too much of a rule orientation can stunt the growth of a relationship. This pattern keeps you from being able to walk in someone else's shoes to tune into their perspective. Usually this type of behavior puts great distance between you and someone else on an emotional level. Your own insights have a tendency to tightly block out those of other individuals. There is too much of a strict adherence to your own belief system when this pattern is activated. The natural, evolving growth of a relationship is stifled. Communication breakdowns usually result when living in the walls of this past life pattern.

Workaholic

This past life pattern can manifest in more than one way. Capricorns can get so focused on work that people can feel neglected. An unwillingness to pay attention to those depending on you due to being totally distracted by work goals could be a problem. Losing that balance between dedication to a job and career might take you from giving time to a lover. Your commitment to work in this pattern excludes a commitment to a relationship.

There is another path this pattern can take, which is trying to work on others to change them into how you want them to fit your own image of them. This is a type of control behavior that weakens the bond you can form with a person. Blocking someone's own autonomy to be their own person usually results in a person revolting against you.

Sad Outlook

If you become entrapped in this past life memory it may influence you to see the flaws in others and leave out their positive traits. Negativity is ruling your perspectives on relationships rather too much. Rather than encouraging growth in someone, you are being too critical. The love you hope for is difficult to attain when you embrace this pattern. This can be a way of sabotaging a relationship to keep it from becoming emotionally closer. There is a tendency in this pattern to use it as a defense mechanism to keep your feelings hidden. You could be questioning the potential of a relationship too quickly without giving it a fair chance to evolve.

Lack of Imagination

This pattern indicates you are too locked into a grounded way of viewing the world. You can get into a predictable routine that works for you but not necessarily for someone else. When this occurs, you could be rejecting the dreams of someone you care about. Your own idealism and intuition might be too tied down to an overused left-brain approach. If this pattern becomes too dominant, it may keep you from supporting the ideas that are outside of your normal way of thinking. Flexibility, when missing, gets in the way of lessening the impact of this past life influence. When you are not willing to reach out and listen to other people's alternative ideas and passions, then your singular perspective keeps this past life pattern too strong.

Scapegoating

This past life energy becomes a shadow force when you want to blame someone else for your problems. It works as a defense mechanism to keep you from taking responsibility for actions that offend people. You will not get the cooperation you need to reach a mutual agreement on important decisions that impact you and people you need on your team. The harmony you long to attain will remain out of reach when you surrender to the impulse to make use of the negative energy embedded in this pattern. There is a stubborn resistance to admitting you are wrong that becomes a regular behavior. This might be due to you trying to be too perfect. Hiding inner feelings of insecurity are another way this pattern emerges.

This is a past life pattern that could be introduced through a person you know. The universe is giving you a preview of a behavior you once displayed in some past lives that you came into this incarnation to transcend. Rather than embodying this shadowy influence from your own past, you have been given an opportunity to first recognize it in another individual. You can then choose not to walk down this same path again.

One Is the Loneliest Number

It is okay if you have decided living alone works for you. But what if a life of solitude is not your first choice? It is very possible that a past life energy is coming between you and settling comfortably into a relationship. The closer someone tries to be to you, there is a tendency for you to pull away. A type of closeness and distance seesaw becomes all too present in your intimate relationships. A lack of trust is at the root of this pattern. Your emotional world is carefully protected to the point of keeping others locked out. Sharing your inner world with someone feels like crossing a vast ocean. Letting someone know you need them is difficult to reveal.

The Cancer Reward for Using Your Sixth Sense Intuitive Perception to Solve Karmic Patterns

It is a magical journey to explore ways to overcome past life patterns. As you begin the path to new self-discovery, it does take some effort along with great patience. If you identify with any of the past life patterns discussed, then chances are they have carried over from more than one past life. The good news is that if you overcome this past life shadow during this incarnation, it balances out all of those past life memories into a positive force.

It might seem like your eyes have a new vision as you awaken to the hold of a past life pattern. Don't be discouraged if you feel like you have taken a step backward in overcoming past life energies. This is a normal part of the process. There will come a time when you will find the inner strength to rise above the hold of a karmic pattern. You will appreciate the renewed sense of personal power. You will enjoy a greater harmony in all of your personal relationships. In letting go of the hold of a past life pattern, it widens the road to finding more fulfillment in your relationships. That first acknowledgment of a past life pattern is the key to opening up a more productive channeling of what was once a negative expression into new positive insights.

The I am the Boss pattern only needs you to understand you don't always have to be in control in your relationships. Allowing room for a loved one to declare their own territory encourages greater trust working for each of you. It actually takes much less energy to have a partner or friend declaring their own independence rather than looking for your approval of their decisions. The bells of harmony ring much louder when you move away from this past life influence. Each time you consciously attempt to let others express their opinions freely, it becomes an automatic way of interacting with people. It is in surrendering the impulse to be bossy that the individuals you want to influence become attracted to your needs.

The Rigid Focus pattern only needs you to take that Capricorn power of concentration you possess and not forget to pay attention to those around you. You can train yourself to listen to the ideas of those you care about. It often makes a plan of action better if you include the insights of individuals you trust. That powerful, focusing talent you can display only needs to slow down and make others feel their own goals are also valued. Flexibility is the key to unlocking the hold of this past life shadow energy. Your mind is energized and gains support from others when you show you can adapt to change. Your relationships increase in love and happiness in walking away from this past life pattern.

The On My Guard pattern is asking you to stop over protecting your feelings if you want to experience love and intimacy on a deeper level. When you reveal some of your emotional nature, it stimulates closeness and trust. You don't need to share all of your secrets but letting someone experience you beyond only an intellectual level forms a stronger lasting bond. Relationships take time to truly get to know someone. It speeds up the process of feeling like you are in a promising relationship when letting someone into your inner world. Showing vulnerability is not a sign of weakness but rather a show of attractive strength.

The Conditional Love pattern is easier to overcome if you loosen up your approach to expressing love for others. You don't need to be setting rules when it comes to showing your warmth toward someone. You will soon realize your relationships are more enjoyable when not making up conditions. Romantic love has a power of its own. The universe has a magical way of giving you pleasant surprises when you don't worry about trying to control outcomes. You are going to receive much more emotional support and love when surrendering conditions imposed on others. This past life influence will be less of a problem when you understand love cannot be conditional and when trusting someone enough to enjoy the shared journey.

Buddha said, "be vigilant, guard your mind against negative thoughts." The Addicted to Negative Thinking pattern needs you to think in a new, invigorated, positive direction. Negativity drains energy whereas when you put your mind in a positive framework it enhances your ability to refrain from judging others as well as yourself. It is true this past life shadow can be linked to being too guided by perfection. It is a trap to be negative because someone is not perfect enough. If you use that wonderful Capricorn focus to channel it into a positive mindset, your relationships become empowered. Better yet those special people you care about join forces with you into a harmony that cannot be denied.

There is a possibility you could come face to face with this pattern through someone else carrying it. Think of it as an opportunity to not walk down the same path as a person you encounter. If you remain traveling in the positive lane, there is less opportunity for this pattern of thinking to infiltrate your perceptions. Each of us will entertain negative thoughts at times, but there is less likelihood you will fall back into repeating this past life pattern if you practice putting your positive instincts to the forefront.

The Weak Assertiveness pattern will need you to take a chance to once in a while throw caution to the wind and boldly make your insights known. It may take some practice if this does not come naturally. You are more likely to enjoy witnessing yourself coming out from behind the curtain and assertively making sure your voice is heard. Your relationships get more balanced when people get a chance to experience your true opinions. When you rise above this past life influence, there is a better chance you will attract partners that have a mutual willingness to listen to your input about major decisions. The leadership instincts in Capricorns come alive when you take that leap of faith to speak from your heart. The fear of revealing your true needs to someone will lessen when you walk out of the shadows of this past life pattern.

The Too Austere pattern is converted from a limiting energy into a more expansive one with a new flexible attitude. You don't need to compromise your own values but do need to create enough space in a relationship for someone to feel mutually accepted. Having a narrow set of expectations when traded in for an openness to another person's need for independence helps a relationship grow. There is an inner sense of knowing boundaries in Capricorn. When not infringing on someone else's territory the harmony becomes a reality. Relinquishing a tendency to hold on to a predetermined agenda allows the universe to deliver a package in a relationship far greater than you imagined.

The Workaholic pattern comes down to finding a balance between work and making a commitment of time to those you love. If you make this a continuing plan, there is a great chance your relationships will stay on an even keel. If you are making sure you listen to the people you care about and support their needs, the happiness you desire will occur. Capricorn gives you an extra dose of devotion to a job. You only need to turn some of that focus to quality time with your special people. You have a great capacity to compartmentalize work and time with a loved one.

Remember to work harder on a problem than a person. It brings someone closer if you let them be themselves. The shared independence in your relationships is what makes being together a true treasure of wealth.

The Sad Outlook pattern needs you to look for the best qualities in others rather than concentrating on their shortcomings. Each of us has areas where there is room for improvement. It is more likely you will find harmony in a relationship when you maintain a positive attitude. It will keep you from falling back into this past life influence. If you do find yourself starting to display this pattern again, don't panic. It will take some practice to walk in a new direction. Rather than leaving a relationship too fast, try giving it a fair chance to evolve. If you take the risk of revealing your deeper feelings you might begin to see you have found someone with whom to share a wealth of happiness.

The Lack of Imagination pattern will not become a repeating past life influence if you open your mind to listening to the hopes and dreams of others. Capricorn gives you a pragmatic and logical mind. When you step out of a too-grounded mental framework, it lets your intuition into the inner world of those you love. You don't have to walk along the same footsteps of someone close to you but do need to accept their own belief system. Supporting the goal of a person you care about, even if it is somewhat out of your normal thinking, brings that person to support your own plans. If you show flexibility, it creates a bridge between you and someone you love that promises fulfillment and a long-lasting trust.

The Scapegoating pattern can be kept from occurring once again in the current incarnation through taking responsibility for your actions. If you refrain from blaming others when life is not going how you want it to, this past life influence stays away. Finding the humility to admit a mistake is the sure way to keep peace and harmony in your relationships. Capricorn can provide you with a persona that projects outer strength. If you come out from behind the mask and show your vulnerability, people find it easier to trust you.

If it is true a person close to you is exhibiting this pattern of behavior, consider it your chance to recognize you don't need to make this thinking part of your own life path. You could have come into this lifetime to shed this past life pattern from your own reality. It is an opportunity to heal this past life memory.

The One Is the Loneliest Number pattern becomes a less lonely life if you are willing to take the risk of trusting someone in an intimate relationship. It may take an act of courage to let your guard down. It is very possible that in some past lives, rejection really hurt. You came here to shake off the influence of this past life shadow. It would only take one very positive experience with a person to send this past life memory packing. There can be caution in Capricorn to release a fear of failure. You may find it easier than you think to open up to a new perspective about relationships. Taking small steps to letting someone into your life will become a bigger path to experiencing joy. Let your intuition guide you forward so the universe can make it possible to find relationship fulfillment.

The Capricorn Reward from Solving Karmic Patterns

There is a tenacity in your sign Capricorn to solve a problem and not give up until the job is finished. That same determination gives you the edge in mastering the challenge presented by any past life pattern. There is the possibility that your mind might tell you that the progress you hoped to make has stalled. If you keep trying to make a conscious effort, eventually you will see how far you have really come. In some ways it is like climbing a mountain. The view from the top makes the journey worth the effort.

If one or more of these karmic patterns seem like part of your reality, don't let it worry you. Each of us has brought past life patterns to work on in this incarnation. The main thing is having the awareness to grow. Patience in trying to heal a past life pattern is good to remember. It does not matter how many past lives you may have repeated a past pattern, if you resolve it in this lifetime it puts all of those past lives in balance.

Maintaining a positive attitude helps overcome a karmic pattern and steer you toward relationship harmony. The possibilities to enjoy love and peace in how you relate to others increase greatly when you gain insight into a past life shadow. Your insights will feel like they have clearer vision and attracting happiness with others will find a new reality.

Capricorn the Ruler Journal Prompts

1. How do you feel when you see the Capricorn image?
2. What Capricorn archetype traits do you resonate most with?
3. What are your career goals?
4. Do you feel older and more mature than others?
5. Do you struggle with expressing your emotions?
6. What do you do for fun?
7. What past life patterns have you experienced?

Chapter Eleven

Aquarius the Outlaw

"I Know"
Keywords: Eccentric, Intelligent, Rebellious, Friendly, Unique, Innovative
Sun Sign Dates: January 20–February 18
Temperament: Sanguine
Sign Type: Air, Fixed
Planetary Ruler: Uranus
Jungian Archetypes: The Outlaw and Rebel
Tarot Card: The Star
Polar Opposite Archetype: The Creator
Astrology Nickname: The Individualist
Polar Opposite Sign: Leo
Symbol: The Water-Bearer
Personality Color: Green, Extroverted
Rules: The Eleventh House, Ankles, Circulatory System

Aquarius Temperament: Sanguine

Aquarius is the eleventh sign of the zodiac. As an air sign you need mental stimulation. You are creative and have a passion for thinking outside the box. Everything you do is different because you like to shock people. You are outgoing and social so having friends is important. People like you and are drawn to your spontaneous and fun-loving nature. You enjoy being a part of groups and spending time with people who share similar interests. You appreciate your freedom and value your independence. As a sanguine personality you get bored easily and need variety in your life. Eccentric, unique, and outgoing you like to stand out from the crowd. You are rebellious and non-traditional in your views. Sometimes forgetful, you can spend a lot of time in deep thought. You like to spend time with people who share similar values but in relationships commitment can be challenging. You are a rebel. Energetic and enthusiastic, you can be the life of the party. Networking and connecting people to the right resource and group makes you feel useful. You need to feel free to make your own decisions and often prefer to just spend time with friends in your spare time. Seeking ways to achieve your hopes, wishes, and dreams inspires you.

Jungian Archetype: The Outlaw

Aquarius is known as the rebel of the zodiac. You like to make your own rules and struggle following other people's regulations. No wonder the outlaw is your archetype. Authority figures can pose difficulties because you prefer doing your own thing. Having independence and being able to express yourself freely in the moment mean a lot to you. As the outlaw archetype you want to push the limits and question tradition. If society says something needs to be a certain way, then you are often the one to step up and question why. You like to do things differently. You like to shock people with how you act, dress, and think. Intelligent and open-minded, you attract many friends from different walks of life. People that are unique, eccentric, and odd are appealing to you. You need to feel alive and like to test the limits. It is important to balance your outlaw nature and learn to live by some of society's rules. If not, you can find yourself in trouble. You can have many acquaintances but can find committed relationships to be difficult unless you are given a lot of space and time alone.

Tarot Card Archetype: The Star

Aquarius is the symbol of the water-bearer. The themes of hope, humanitarian ideals and faith in the future are associated with this card. As an Aquarius, you like to focus on accumulating knowledge, socializing, and networking. Being creative, innovative, and coming up with revolutionary ideas is where you shine. You might be good at science, technology, and enjoy working with computers. The Star is similar to your mission as a visionary who wants to awaken and focus on the future. You prefer non-traditional ideas because you like to maintain a sense of individuality. You have an ability to bring your creativity and intellectual knowledge together to solve problems. In the Star card the person has one foot on the ground and one in the water. This symbolizes grounding your visionary and idealistic views with realism. Balance is the key for you to attain higher wisdom. You can't always have your head in the clouds but need to bring yourself down to earth on occasion.

Sign Type: Air Element

Aquarius is an air sign, and you are known for being highly inventive and a free thinker. You are a bit aloof and emotionally distant at times. Intimacy and relationships can be challenging. You need a mental connection with someone in order to feel attraction. Analyzing and problem solving come naturally. Because of your desire to be different from others, you can act out and rebel. You like to have autonomy and want to be on your own schedule. Bored easily, you need intellectual stimulation. You are restless, spontaneous, and always on the go. Learning new things and exploring the world bring comfort. Futuristic ideas that are innovative such as AI, robots, aliens, and space travel appeal to you. Even though you are unconventional and a nonconformist, there is also a side of you that can be strongly set in your beliefs. You are friendly, social, and fun. Leading groups of people to rebel against things that are seen to be confining or unfair is common. Being open-minded about other people's lifestyles and beliefs is a gift.

Personality Color: Green

Aquarius is similar to the green personality. As a green you are intellectual and have a creative mind. You value information, facts, figures, and knowledge. You might feel uncomfortable making decisions based on emotion. Over-analyzing and rationalizing your feelings can make it difficult for others to understand you. You prefer to study and research things before you make a decision. You're interested in data, facts, and real solutions. Because of your curiosity, you don't just accept things for how they are. You want to question rules, especially when they aren't logical. You are a visionary and deep thinker which can lead to amazing ideas. Too much structure and rules can make you reject the status quo. You like to shake things up, bring change, and help people think differently.

The Aquarius Current Life Relationship Landscape

If you were born under the sign of Aquarius your relationships often begin in surprising ways. You lean toward the unconventional but can enter relationships with individuals whose values differ from your own. It is that unpredictable side of you that some people find attractive and others are not wanting to enter. The traditional astrology phrase for Aquarius is "I invent." You do tend to have a wide variety of social contacts. There is that inner drive to find a soul mate to mutually share your life adventures.

Your mind likely works fast. People who don't expect you to make decisions faster than you prefer to make are appreciated. There is a stubborn resistance to change that is not on your own terms.

You may hold back your feelings until you really trust someone. Your intellect can hold back emotions like a strong dam. That intuitive side of you stays clear if your relationships don't worry you. Independent individuals excite you. They stimulate your creative imagination. You enjoy someone who supports your goals and does not depend on you too heavily too much of the time.

You can grow impatient with people who seem to be holding back the truth from you. Some will not perceive your emotional sensitivity right away. Your thought-provoking mind might conceal your feelings.

Anger at times makes you nervous. You prefer rational individuals who like to solve problems logically. If there is an angry disagreement you want it to be over quickly. You likely don't want to waste time disagreeing about small details.

Your freedom is a big deal. Having your space to reflect and process is a major need. You like people who are not afraid to pursue a dream and will not interfere with your own.

The Aquarius Past Life Karmic Relationship Patterns

Don't be disturbed if you identify with any of the past life patterns that will be discussed. Think of this as a learning experience. Everyone has issues that can surface once again from past lifetimes. Those memories are residing in our consciousness. The main thing to remember is that the information in this book is there to empower you and open up paths to greater relationship fulfillment. Your first steps to look for more ways to express energies through new insights might become awakened.

As an Aquarius, your mental determination may be able to break new ground with any past life patterns. It does take practice and patience when trying to change a behavior. If you hold on to that forward vision you possess, it could surprise you how fast you can turn a negative past life theme into a positive. That desire to attract the right people and abundance into your life is closer than you may think.

Different Just to Be Different

If this past life pattern followed you into this incarnation, it expresses as purposely taking the opposite point of view.

There is a self-orientation to get your own way. There is little thought of trying to really reach a mutual understanding. The root of this past life influence could be hidden anger. Rather than communicating directly about what you need, there is an urge to be contradictory. This pattern does not serve you well in having close relationships based on trust. You are not listening to someone to truly understand their own needs.

Escape into the Future

This past life pattern, if activated, finds you not wanting to deal with issues in the present. Your mind is so much on the future that a lover or friend might wonder if they can count on you when a situation calls for this. Aquarius is a goal-oriented sign. It is only when those future plans get you to ignore the goals of someone close to you that there is a problem. You could be perceived as irresponsible, while you see this as an eagerness to pursue your dreams. If you fail to let others in on your restless search for the promise of tomorrow it causes confusion. The underlying cause of this pattern may be linked to a fear of adversity. Rather than dealing with daily routines, the excitement of the future is constantly calling to you.

Life in the Fast Lane

Your sign is one of the faster moving intellectual signs. It can be a challenge for people to stay on the same page with you when you suddenly want to change directions. It is when you stay unpredictable that this past life pattern grows in intensity. Stability in a relationship could be difficult to attain. The adrenaline rush of constantly wanting to start new endeavors can create turmoil with those you love. Living for the excitement outweighs wanting to be in a committed relationship. Not paying enough attention to the needs of others causes them to hold back on supporting your goals.

I Think Therefore I Am

The mental processes come so automatically to an Aquarius it is like being in cruise control while driving. Crossing over into the emotional lane is difficult when this pattern emerges. If you are reluctant to express any feelings, people closest to you may perceive you as uncaring. This pattern can be well hidden from your conscious memory. It might come as a surprise if someone lets you know that your emotional communication is lacking. This pattern can be a defense mechanism to conceal your inner world from others. It does create a challenge to give others a read on how you really feel about situations that arise.

It is possible this pattern makes an appearance through a person you have met. It may be you have managed to steer clear of this past life shadow in this incarnation. You just need to maintain your clarity and not get pulled into it.

Derailing the Goals of Others

A signal this past life pattern has become a player in your life is if you negate the goals of others too much of the time. There is a tendency to show a lack of faith in individuals needing your positive support. People can feel discounted when you are not getting behind their plans. A resentment starts to unfold, causing others not to give you the support you need. This pattern, if it becomes a regular occurrence, alienates the very people you hope to remain close to. Sometimes this past life shadow will show itself if you are uncomfortable with a relationship partner wanting to come closer. This is your way of distancing yourself.

Don't Crowd Me

There is an instinctual need for freedom built into the sign Aquarius. If you get too set on having space in a moment's notice, it can catch those trying to get close to you off guard. The need to roam freely with no boundaries can be a big ask of your lovers and friends. Some people may perceive you as aloof while you feel this is you being yourself. If you are unreasonable in your need for space it is going to be seen as pushing people away. A failure to communicate the need for some room to breathe clearly causes confusion in your relationships. You could be looked at as too invisible when someone needs you. A commitment is difficult to maintain if you choose to live like an individual with little awareness that you truly want to create a partnership.

Lost in a Cause

There can be a tendency to feel a great allegiance to a group with a shared cause. This pattern can manifest if you are so dedicated to influences outside of your relationship that you ignore a partner. This could be a past life tendency that you are repeating. A lover or soul mate will begin to resent the time taken away from the relationship if you seem to be missing in action. It is when you treat a group or cause as your lover that it can create a sense of separation in a relationship. It can put great stress on a relationship when there is a lack of balance in juggling what you feel you need from pursuing a cause with what you need from a lover. It isn't that you can't live in both worlds. It is that it does not work when someone close to you feels left out of a big chunk of your life. People who love you want to know you will make time for them. They want to know you need them.

Not Learning from the Past

Having your mind on tomorrow more than today is sometimes part of the normal Aquarius business-as-usual thinking. This past life influence could find you bored with the present. Dealing with everyday life can seem bothersome. There may be an attitude that issues in a relationship disappear if you escape into dreaming about future plans. You could keep repeating behaviors over and over that cause friction with others, no matter how much they point this out. A stubborn refusal to compromise causes great lack of cooperation from others. This past life shadow is keeping you from learning from past mistakes made in relationships in this life and from past incarnations.

Extreme Impatience

A sign that this past life pattern could be too much a part of your self-expression is thinking that everyone in your life moves too slowly. Your brain, to others, could seem like a fast-moving taxi driver in a large city changing lanes in a hurry. It does cause tension in your relationships if you show impatience on a regular basis. It will appear to others that your way of getting things done is more important than their way. This usually results in arguments and hurt feelings. Being born as an Aquarius does indicate your mind has the potential to be three steps out in front of other people. When you don't slow down enough, you can end up losing individuals you need in your life.

It is possible that this pattern can show up in your life through a person you have grown close to. It is an opportunity to get a glimpse of this past life shadow in someone else. The key thing is not to walk down this path yourself.

Fear of Change

If this past life pattern awakens, your resistance to change can disrupt the flow in your relationships. Being glued to fixed positions can alienate the people you are trying to keep close. Aquarius can be one of those astrological signs that want to have things on their own terms. If you latch on too tightly to this type of thinking, it can be difficult to adjust to changes in a relationship that a partner might perceive as needed. This past life theme often slips into the current incarnation when you don't trust the motives of another person. Or it can simply be you are wanting to remain in what you think are your own comfort zones. Being able to let yourself reach a mutual agreement with someone is a real challenge. You could be expecting others to do all the compromising, which usually puts a great deal of distance between you and a person with whom you hope to have a feeling of harmony.

Loss of Independence

This past life pattern, when entering your current incarnation, could show you attracting strong-minded individuals that overshadow your feelings of thinking for yourself. This runs contrary to that independent streak that travels through the mind of an Aquarius. Your own goals in this type of relationship often get put on hold to meet the needs of others. Your natural drive to find equality in a relationship is stalled if you are too compromising. Emotional confusion usually results if you stay locked into this past life influence. Your assertiveness becomes too watered down in tiptoeing around those you are trying too hard to please. That equality you require to express your true voice is drowned out by someone not considering your own life pursuits.

Too Close for Comfort

If this past life pattern becomes active, you find the greater the distance with a lover the better off you feel. It can be a carryover from past lives where a fear of abandonment was an issue. It makes it a challenge to open up emotionally if you find closeness makes you extremely uncomfortable. Most Aquarians prefer enough space in a relationship to feel like they can be themselves. The problem if this past life shadow presents is that there is never enough space to make you feel at ease with someone. A fear of a relationship ending with hurtful feelings could be another reason this pattern has emerged. Your unwillingness to talk about your anxiety about the fear of intimacy with a lover may keep this past life theme a problem.

The Aquarius Reward for Using Your Sixth Sense Intuitive Perceptions to Solve Karmic Patterns

There will be a great sense of relief when you work your way through a past life pattern. The effort you make pays great dividends. Your mind will feel a new inspiration to express the knowledge gained in bringing a past life shadow out into the light. Your relationships offer greater fulfillment when you make a bold statement in facing a past life karmic influence. Courageously rising above the fog presented by a past life pattern puts you on the road to relationship harmony.

Remember it takes patience and practice to navigate through these past life memories that are still with you in this incarnation. There is no need to judge yourself if you feel a connection to any of these past life patterns. Think of it as a learning experience along a journey of self-discovery. Don't be surprised if you take one step forward and two backward. It is an evolutionary process that as you travel along it will reveal exciting new clarity. With each new insight your confidence will grow. Each of us has lessons to learn in our current life. You will realize, as you gain increasing awareness of a pattern, that it becomes easier to not let it come between you and those you love.

The Different Just to Be Different pattern can be resolved by thinking in terms of win-win solutions. If you realize that your uniqueness is what people are often attracted to, there is no need to go to extremes. You will find the closeness you hope to create with someone flows smoothly when you show you value the insights of others. You don't have to always agree with someone expressing their own perspective. If you are making an attempt to listen to others, it is a positive step to greater harmony in your relationships. Aquarius gives you a natural rebellious and freedom streak. Nobody can really take this away from you. Sharing your knowledge with others stimulates them to trust you and their willingness to give you the space you need is more likely to occur.

The Escape into the Future pattern is lessened in its intensity when you balance what is expected of you in the present with the call of the future. Your Sun sign Aquarius will regularly get you to look forward when putting a plan into motion. If you can remember to communicate clearly with those wanting to be included in your everyday life, this past life pattern will not be a problem. Dealing with issues as they occur actually frees you to put your energy into your favorite pastimes. Facing adversity with a lover deepens the trust in the relationship. You may be surprised to learn that a problem is not as big as it seemed when talking it through with someone. Taking the time to share ideas in tackling an issue is a way to achieve a feeling of togetherness.

The Life in the Fast Lane pattern is easier to handle when you don't get in too much of a hurry on a regular basis. It is easy to think everyone else has a speedy mind that doesn't need a lot of time to process life experiences. There is a side of Aquarius you can go to, when needed, that can find a slower rhythm. You can show a great ability to focus on the goals that you highly value. When you let others in on your thought processes it doesn't shock them with sudden surprise. You do possess sharp communication skills. Intimacy and trust build as a foundation in your relationships when you pay attention to what people need from you. Sometimes it is pausing just long enough to notice the little things that make someone happy, that sees them traveling in a lane of joy right alongside of you.

The I Think Therefore I Am pattern only needs for you to come out from a well-defined mental fortress and show your feelings. People find you easier to understand when you show your emotions. Revealing your inner world might take some time but in doing so a lover can experience you on a deeper level. Your mental nature likes to connect with a person through words and concepts. This makes a great way to enter a relationship. If you find the courage to let those words carry your feelings, you will open the door to relationship fulfillment.

This pattern may have come into your life expressed through a person you are involved with in a relationship. Try to realize this is an opportunity to get a view of this pattern and an opportunity to not accept this past life shadow into your own reality.

The Derailing the Goals of Others pattern is turned around quickly by dropping a negative attitude when someone needs positive support from you. The chances of creating a harmonious relationship increase greatly when you show you care about the success of a loved one's plan. The flow of love and an equal exchange of positive encouragement for goals is enhanced with less criticism. You don't have to agree on everything. But you will find your relationships are more fulfilling when you offer helpful insights to those who need it from you. When you show you are paying attention and honoring the dreams of someone else, chances are they want to remain close to you. This past life shadow that has followed you into this incarnation is not going to get activated when you offer your most loving support to a person you care about.

The Don't Crowd Me pattern is less problematic if you understand you need to communicate your freedom needs clearly. Generally speaking, Aquarians like yourself appreciate a lot of breathing room in relationships. If you act responsibly and really participate actively with a lover, you likely will be granted the freedom you require. The main thing to remember is that the important people in your life want to know you will be there when needed. A key way to keep this past life pattern completely dormant is to have some shared activities with people you love and want to maintain closeness. It is a sure way to get the private time you need. There is a good chance a partner will appreciate some alone time for themselves. Time to yourself is not a problem when people in your life know they are never far from your thoughts and heart.

The Lost in a Cause pattern lessens in its influence when you show enough flexibility by not dedicating all of yourself to a group or cause. It is okay if it stimulates your mind to connect with a group. It is important to keep this pattern from playing the trickster and occupying too much of your time and not ignoring the people you depend on in your life. It is essential you consciously allot time to a relationship to keep it growing. Being an Aquarius, you can have great focus when you feel passionate about a cause. The key thing to remember is to not let the pursuit of a group identity or a cause become more important than the love you feel for someone close to you. Making a genuine effort to spend quality time with a special person is a clear way to rise above this past life pattern.

The Not Learning from the Past pattern is easier to manage when you make a concerted effort to deal with present issues in a relationship. Your mind will always, to some degree, likely be thinking about what steps to take to accomplish future goals. When you show you are remembering not to repeat behaviors that anger others, this pattern fades far into the background. Being willing to adapt to change in a relationship is a sure way to send this pattern out of your life. The past is a great teacher when we learn not to repeat actions that disrupt the peace in a relationship. There are new insights that can be gained in accepting the reality that working in a spirit of cooperation with those you love is the path to great harmony.

The Extreme Impatience pattern is easier to resolve if you take the time to get some input from a partner or close friend before speeding ahead on an idea. Getting some insight from someone else to compare with your own is one way to let a person know you value their opinion. Chances are people know that in the end you will make your own independent choices. It is just like magic in conquering this past life pattern when you pay attention to an individual close to you. It then does not really matter if you happen to be one of those fast-thinking and quick-to-act Aquarians. There is an objective and reflective dimension to Aquarius that comes into play when you slow down. It never hurts to pause and consider how your fast pace is impacting those around you. When you include the special people in your life in a plan, you are more apt to get the support and encouragement you would love to have.

If this pattern is coming at you through someone else in your life, it is the universe giving you a preview of the impact of this behavior. Consider it an opportunity to be a watcher of this pattern rather than a player in it. It could be a karmic pattern you came into this life not to engage in once again.

The Fear of Change pattern is one that challenges you to be more flexible. When you are able to do so, life with others has a flowing atmosphere. Intimacy comes naturally and the love given and received is a great feeling. Letting go of very fixed ways of doing things makes it easier to dance with the minds of others in a shared rhythm. When you step out of your own comfort zones now and then, it is easier to walk into the comfort zones of others and enjoy the experience. It is more likely someone will then be more accepting of your own likes and dislikes. Trust between you and the people you want to establish closeness with becomes easier when you show a willingness to be open to new ideas.

The Loss of Independence pattern is overcome by not fearing the need to walk to your own drumbeat. Those initial quiet steps to being more assertive will eventually be followed by louder ones. A feeling of independence is the oxygen an Aquarian must experience to feel confident. Staying clear of those people who are too controlling may be needed. You thrive on relationships that are based on equality. When you're not the only one compromising, it strengthens you mentally and emotionally. Your natural instincts are to desire an equal give and take in relationships. Your goals in life feel empowered when you are in a partnership with someone you trust. It is then you fly like a free eagle and this past life pattern is no longer an influence in the current life.

The Too Close for Comfort pattern is needing you to take the risk of trusting someone enough to come closer. Usually the fear of something is worse than the actual experience. This past life influence will lessen in its interference when you communicate honestly with someone. Aquarius is a strong, intellectual sign. If you allow your emotions to be expressed, closeness becomes more comfortable. It takes retraining your mind to allow feelings to come through you to a lover. Trust is the key to overcoming this pattern. You need to believe that you are strong enough to allow a person to get to know you on a deeper level. Don't worry if this feels awkward at first. It will take some practice. The effort will pay off in that it creates a bridge to greater intimacy and harmony.

The Aquarius Reward from Solving Karmic Patterns

The long-range vision of Aquarius is hard to match by any other astrological sign. The ruling planet of Aquarius is Uranus. This planet orbits in a unique way, sitting on its side while all of the other planets orbit in a straight up and down movement. Likewise, the sign Aquarius can display a laser-like insight in rising above any karmic pattern. It will take steady focus and consistent effort to outlast the influence of a past life shadow. Each step along the journey does produce more confidence as you gain a foothold in walking away from past life patterns that have possibly interfered with your relationship happiness.

The Rolling Stones song, "Get Off of My Cloud" is sometimes how you may feel in wanting to walk to the sound of your own drumbeat. Your innate ability to break free from the hold of a past life influence helps you gain a new sense of self-discovery.

Be patient as you gain greater awareness of any karmic pattern. Enjoy the growth and fulfillment that can come your way as you move into new insights. The reward for walking on the road that is often less traveled brings you into the light of personal and relationship harmony.

Aquarius the Outlaw Journal Prompts

1. How do you feel when you see the Aquarius image?
2. What Aquarius archetype traits do you resonate most with?
3. In what ways do you like to stand out?
4. What are your creative talents?
5. Do you struggle with committed relationships?
6. Do you enjoy being a part of groups?
7. What past life patterns have you experienced?

Chapter Twelve

Pisces the Innocent

"I Believe"
Keywords: Idealistic, Compassionate, Romantic, Artistic, Imaginative, Spiritual
Sun Sign Dates: February 19–March 20
Temperament: Phlegmatic
Sign Type: Water, Mutable
Planetary Ruler: Neptune
Jungian Archetype: The Innocent
Tarot Card: The Moon
Polar Opposite Archetype: The Sage
Astrology Nickname: The Mystic
Polar Opposite Sign: Virgo
Symbol: The Fishes
Personality Color: Blue, Introverted
Rules: The Twelfth House, Feet

Pisces Temperament: Phlegmatic

Pisces is the twelfth sign of the zodiac. You are compassionate and intuitive. Sensitive, emotional, and spiritual you care about helping others. Having strong boundaries will help you in many areas of your life. Because you are an empath, you get your own feelings confused with other people's. Your idealism can make it easy for you to see the good in other people. You wear rose-colored glasses and put people up on a pedestal. Sometimes you sacrifice your own life for others and find it hard to stay no. Pisces is a phlegmatic personality and needs to connect to other people. Being in love and experiencing romance helps you feel alive. Finding a spiritual path and connection is important for you to feel grounded. You like to escape from the world and need your solitude. Being alone helps you heal and recover from the stress in the world. You need to balance your emotions and practical responsibilities. It is important that you serve others in some way, and you are interested in astrology, social work, and psychology.

Jungian Archetype: The Innocent

As compassionate and sensitive souls, Pisceans are considered the mystics of the zodiac. You are known to be extremely trusting and naïve. Just like the innocent personality, you see the world with rose-colored glasses. You are idealistic and see the best in people. Being able to help people with their problems gives you a sense of purpose.

You enjoy creative and artistic pursuits. Music soothes your soul, and you may have artistic talents. Expressing your feelings in creative ways helps you heal. Because of your emotional sensitivity it's key that you learn to be more realistic about other people's motives. Trust your gut instinct and don't second guess yourself. There are times you may feel betrayed, used, or taken advantage of. Your innocent and trusting nature needs to be protected. Try to develop stronger boundaries and this will help you succeed in many areas of life. You may be prone to emotional lows and depression. These feelings of sadness might make you want to escape from your problems. The stress of practical responsibilities can be overwhelming. Be cautious about drinking too much or getting caught up in addictive behaviors. Don't lose your kindness after people hurt you but learn to guard your heart.

Tarot Card Archetype: The Moon

The Moon tarot card is associated with Pisces. The moon in astrology rules the emotions. You are psychic and often get glimpses of the future through your dreams. Instinctual things seem to come into your mind and it's like you know what other people are feeling. The moon symbolism reminds you to trust your intuition. Helping others alleviate their emotional pain through caring for and listening to their problems can bring fulfillment. The cycles of the moon related to this card are about growth and healing. Your compassion and sensitivity to the environment can make it difficult for you to protect yourself. Having strong boundaries and listening to your gut instinct can help. Ground your energy and process your emotions so that you can feel balanced. You might experience strong feelings and, at times, depression. On one hand you enjoy your private time alone, and yet you can also feel lonely. It is a healthy outlet for you to be creative and express your artistic abilities. Listening to music can be healing and help you connect.

Element: Water

It's no surprise that Pisces is a water sign. You are deep, intuitive, and psychic. You have a knack for picking up on other people's energy and can be clairvoyant. Because you are a water sign there is a heightened sensitivity to the environment. You might dream about the future and get psychic messages through meditation. You are an empath and can feel other people's pain. Trust your feelings because they are often right. People like to open up to you and share their problems. You are a natural counselor and able to make others feel supported. There are times you feel sad for no reason and you can withdraw from others and seek solitude. Sometimes you might feel lonely or want to escape. Spending time near the ocean or near water can help you balance your energy.

Personality Color: Blue

Pisces personality traits are similar to the blue personality. You like to feel needed, appreciated and enjoy helping others.

Working on relationships and finding true love are important to you. You are a great listener and very supportive of those you care about. Extremely intuitive and caring, you try hard to bring peace into your environment. Born with natural people skills, you excel in career fields where you can help others with their problems. You might want to work as a teacher, counselor, nurse, or as an astrologer. You can be extra sensitive to criticism and tend to get your feelings hurt easily. If you develop stronger boundaries and learn not to take things so personally it will help. It is important to remember that it's not your job to save the world. It's not easy for you to tell other people no, but developing healthy relationships will help you find greater emotional balance. Sometimes self-protection is needed in order to surround yourself with positive people who are a good influence.

The Pisces Current Life Relationship Landscape

If you were born under the sign Pisces your mental and emotional energies like to ride alongside of themselves. The traditional astrology slogan for Pisces is "I believe." This implies you like to have dreams and ideals that inspire you. People who can accept this part of your identity are welcomed and those who don't have a more difficult time understanding you. It isn't that you are not reality-oriented. Your ambition has to be fueled by passion and some degree of emotional award. Individuals loving you the way you are make it easier to form a close relationship with them.

Your closest lovers and friends might share your love of the arts. You are generous to those you feel deserving of your generosity. Individuals who lean on you too heavily for emotional or material support can be draining. Knowing your boundaries comes with experience. Guilt is something you have to overcome. You realize sooner or later you can't please everyone all of the time.

Falling in love is a powerful spiritual experience for you. Searching for a soul mate is an innate desire. Knowing who to trust is a learning process. When you find the right person, it will be like they can read you without your speaking. But there are times when people will ask you to speak your mind.

Meeting new friends or lovers might seem like a magical synchronicity created by the universe. You like individuals with a belief system that makes sense to you. Someone giving you confidence through believing in you captures your heart.

You don't have much use for people bringing unneeded stress into your life. Peace and quiet are preferred over exhausting arguments. Your privacy is sacred and must be respected. You don't want to be controlled by anyone but do want an intimacy you can trust. You have a natural feeling of compassion for those you care about. You will fight to protect your beliefs and what you love.

The Pisces Past Life Karmic Relationship Patterns

If you connect with any of the past life patterns that will be discussed, don't let it bother you. The idea is to gain greater awareness about past life influences and to get a more positive expression in dealing with them. Each of us has brought in past life shadow energies we are trying to bring out into the light of clarity. Think of it as an evolutionary journey. So, remember there is no need to judge yourself. It is an evolving learning process.

As a Pisces, your faith in your ability to rise above a karmic pattern is within your reach at all times. The road to greater relationship harmony becomes clearer in acknowledging one of these patterns. It takes practice and patience so don't get discouraged if you find yourself falling back into a past life thought pattern. These memories from past incarnations can be healed in this lifetime. Don't worry about being too perfect. It can seem messy as you begin the path to transcending the hold of a past life pattern. Just keep moving forward and before you know it you will perceive your new growth. Self-discovery is exciting.

Don't Make Any Waves

This pattern makes itself known if you fear facing adversity in a relationship. There is a tendency to hide your displeasure with someone's actions thinking it will maintain peace and quiet. The issues you have with someone don't go away. Pisces is a water sign that can find you wanting things to always flow smoothly with others. A failure to communicate what you need from a person does eventually lead to frustration for both of you. Enabling the behavior that you find bothersome to continue without pointing this out causes anger to build. Your moods can suddenly swing to extremes as your emotional intensity builds in this pattern. Defining a relationship clearly becomes a major challenge.

Helpless Victim

Dependency needs get out of balance if this past life pattern gets activated. You can find yourself having unrealistic expectations for emotional support that begin to drain the energy of others. If you are always needing to be saved from situations you have found yourself in, it begins to put tremendous strain on a relationship. This pattern is often caused by a lack of clarity in what you want from a relationship. In not taking enough responsibility for important decisions that are needed in a relationship it can result in frustration for each of you. You are relinquishing too much control to someone else. Your own sense of personal power is being overly limited.

This past life influence can show up through a lover constantly acting helpless to get attention. It might be a pattern you have come into this life to overcome and getting revealed to you through a person you know intimately. It is your opportunity to perceive this pattern clearly before you embrace it for yourself.

Love Is Blind

You could be in a relationship where your boundaries are very blurred. The idealism of Pisces is sometimes way out in front of the reality. In this past life pattern you might be superimposing your imagination onto someone and believing that a partner can do no wrong. Falling in love is a powerful, emotional experience. If this pattern gets activated from your past life memory you may have trouble being objective about someone. It is possible your own needs could become lost in trying to fulfill whatever a lover wants from you. Entering relationships too fast without giving it some time to make sure a person is who they seem to be causes this past life shadow to grow stronger.

Emotional Rescuer

A signal this past life pattern has been activated is if you feel you must always fix the problems of others. Your boundaries get lost in an emotional fog. You can't really save someone from having to deal with their problems. Your good intentions may be prolonging an issue for a person in that they keep repeating it. You probably become disappointed with someone replicating the same behavior over and over again that you are trying to fix. This is offering emotional support but having expectations that are unreasonable. This pattern can become a bad habit in thinking you must assume the responsibility for the problems created by others.

Looking for Perfection

There are no perfect people. But if you fall into this past life pattern your mind can become too attached to looking for a perfect partner. It puts a lot of pressure on you and someone else to live up to unrealistic expectations. There will always be divine discontent embedded in this pattern, meaning you will keep finding flaws in a person. It makes forming a solid relationship next to impossible. This is accepting a self-imposed mission that is truly a tall mountain to climb. To stay on this path only results in disappointment.

This pattern you came into this incarnation to gain clarity about could be presented through someone expecting too much perfection from you. This will sooner or later be realized as expectations you cannot fulfill. Think of this as the universe showing you a behavior you don't want to make part of your own thinking in this incarnation.

Cold Feet

If this past life pattern becomes too much of a player in your life, it can be difficult to make a serious commitment to a relationship. You may have met someone who seems like the right partner for you. But as the person wants to get to know you on a deeper level, it causes you to pull back. It may puzzle you why this keeps occurring in your relationships. Embedded in your mind are past life memories where you could have had trouble with trust due to emotional pain. You can't seem to break through the hesitation and establish a long stable relationship. If you are happy with living alone this is no problem. If you want to live with a lover in a committed relationship, this pattern is troublesome.

Running from Adversity

Pisces can be a super-sensitive sign. You can feel the energy of people in a room more than they realize. It is this same tuning into the feelings of others that can cause this past life pattern to emerge. You anticipate the coming friction over an issue with someone, but your first impulse is to avoid dealing with the problem. Usually what you are choosing to escape from only enlarges your differences with people. The distance emotionally between you and a lover becomes a vast ocean if you don't communicate more openly. Every relationship, no matter how wonderful, will have a bit of conflict. This is a past life shadow that, if not dealt with at some point, can cause you to miss out on good relationships that have a promise of harmony.

Sounds of Silence

There are times when being quiet and reflective is good for the mind. Then there are instances when people need to hear what is in your thoughts. If this past life pattern is too active in your life you can become too withdrawn. If you become too invisible when your input is needed the important people in your life will perceive this as an avoidance behavior. When you expect someone to read your mind it can result in confusion. It may be thought that your silence is a disapproval of someone's ideas or actions. In leaving too much up for interpretation and not communicating, it causes distance from those you want to bring closer. Pisces is a water sign that at times retreats to recharge the mental energies. In its extreme form, it can leave you absent from having a vibrant presence in a relationship. If that is the case, it reveals that this pattern occupies too big a part of your thought processes.

Paradise Lost

If this past life pattern becomes activated there is a tendency to look for the negative in others without even trying to notice the positive. It could be from a memory linked to some past lives from relationships that did not live up to your expectations. Your mental filters are too stuck on losing faith in the belief that you will not find a person that makes you feel happy. There is a side of Pisces that is a true romantic. Falling in love may feel good to you. It is accepting the day-to-day living with someone that worries you. Life can get messy, and issues do arise. If you remain fixed on the idea that you can find a relationship without ever having to face some adversity, then this pattern becomes too much a part of your reality.

Coloring the Truth

This past life influence finds you telling people what you think they want to hear. It may be twisting the truth to keep someone liking you. It may be a way of manipulating situations to get what you feel you need from a person. Your negotiations with individuals are more like business transactions than on an emotional level. Trust is often lacking in this pattern. You don't really want to let anyone into your inner world. You are more comfortable staying on the level of presenting a persona to others, masking your fear of a true intimacy. Overly residing in the walls of this past life shadow prevents you from obtaining a deeper, fulfilling love.

Comparison Shopping

This past life pattern could find you searching over and over again for a person who reminds you of a past lover. It does present a challenge as finding someone who is the perfect replacement is impossible. Not letting go of a lover from the past makes it difficult to create enough room for a new person to enter your life. There is another way this pattern can become activated. It is possible this pattern may be connected to a past life relationship that is locked in your memory that has you seeking someone who perfectly matches the qualities of that past life lover. It will keep you frustrated, looking for someone dominating your imagination that may never appear.

My Truth Is the Truth

You become too particular on how you like things done when this past life pattern has gained too much strength. People will perceive you as too uncompromising. It might be that your mind has trouble considering other options to your own ideas. Inflexibility tends to alienate the people you want to support your goals. Closeness turns quickly into distance if you rigidly hold on to your own opinions. Rather than operating as an open-minded team player it could put you into a solo act as others feel pushed away.

The Pisces Reward for Using Your Sixth Sense Intuitive Perception to Solve Karmic Patterns

When overcoming a karmic pattern, it frees you in several ways. You can attain a more optimistic attitude about relationships. A new vitality can feel like it has occurred. What was once a shadow from a past life interfering with your relationship happiness has now disappeared. The effort to move beyond the negative gravity of a past life influence is well worth the struggle. It is easier to attract the right people into your life when you've moved beyond a past life energy.

If you identified with any of the karmic patterns that were discussed, try not to let it worry you. Each of us has brought some past life experiences into the current incarnation that we are trying to gain insight into. Think of this as a path of self-discovery. The opportunity to explore an alternative way to express a past life energy opens new doors to relationship harmony. Those first awakenings about past life patterns can stimulate your mind into productive, life-changing perceptions. The growth along this journey can feel exciting. You will likely come to the realization that there is no turning back. The path forward will call to you to keep seeking greater understanding of any past life pattern.

The Don't Make Any Waves pattern is less of an echo in your mind if you take the first steps to be more assertive. People assume you don't mind their treatment of you if you fail to speak up. It could seem awkward at first to say what you have been holding back. With practice it does get easier. Your relationships stay in balance when you voice your opinions openly. Anger has less of a chance to build if you communicate your thoughts. Your insights get empowered as you let others hear them. Your mind, body and spirit find their natural alignment as you verbalize your ideas. Harmony in your relationships resonates in engaging with others in lively discussions.

The Helpless Victim pattern requires you to get your dependency needs balanced. You don't need to take on all the responsibility for decisions in a relationship; you only need to focus on pulling your own weight. Think in terms of equality and you are most of the way there in overcoming this past life shadow. Tuning in to your own personal power attracts the right types of people into your life to experience fulfillment. Paying attention to what others need makes it more likely they will do the same for you. Your relationships receive rays of harmony when you don't always lean too heavily on others for emotional support.

If you are in a relationship with a person exhibiting this pattern, consider it a preview of a behavior you came into this lifetime not to accept. The universe is showing you a past life influence you need to recognize but not embrace.

The Love is Blind pattern is lessened in its influence when you take the time to reality test relationships. Slow down and make sure that what your imagination is telling you about a person is real. You need to define your boundaries clearly. Pisces' emotions grow strong when falling in love. There is nothing wrong with this. Just make sure you keep your objectivity tuned up because it helps keep your eyes open in a clearer way. Love and logic don't seem like they belong together when it comes to romance. But they are both needed to keep this past life influence from manifesting in this incarnation.

The Emotional Rescuer pattern is less likely to trouble you when you learn to step back from always coming to the rescue of others. It is better not to enable someone to keep getting into the same problems over and over again by thinking you are required to make everything right. It empowers you and those you care about to let them deal with their issues. You can be a supportive friend and lover without trying to assume all of the responsibility. It is a needed learning experience to let someone face their challenges and even gain wisdom from mistakes made. It is exhausting thinking you must be the rescuer. Your own mental strength gets drained less when overcoming this past life tendency. The big payoff is that your relationships will become more enjoyable and fulfilling.

The Looking for Perfection pattern is easier to navigate if you set your expectations to be more realistic. The harder you try to change someone into an image that resembles perfection in your mind, the more that person is likely to resist changing just to please you. If you accept a flexible attitude, the happier you will be. Letting go of trying to control or manipulate a person to fit into an idealized portrait of what you think they should be is a better path. Creating a relationship with someone yields a much better composite or sense of unity. There is always some compromise in every successful partnership, whether a business or a romantic one. The universe has a better chance to give you a harmonious relationship when you put away the perfect script in favor of a magical, surprising one.

There is the chance you can encounter a person who portrays this pattern that you came into this life to overcome. This would be your opportunity to perceive this behavior as something you don't want to accept as part of your own reality.

Pisces in astrology rules the feet. You don't need to have cold ones when it comes to the Cold Feet pattern. Taking the risk of letting someone get to know you on an emotional level does allow a deeper intimacy to form. You don't need to move too fast into a new relationship. Giving it time to develop is one way to take the fear out of closeness. You need to convince yourself you have much to offer in a relationship. Look at the relationship experience as a journey. It usually takes time for the depth to reveal itself. If you never take a chance on someone, you will never know if you have found the right partner. Chances are someone you meet has their own fears. The key thing to remember in shaking loose from this past life pattern is to trust yourself. The fear is usually worse than getting to know someone and learning how to have an enjoyable shared experience of each other.

The Running from Adversity pattern can be turned around by realizing your sensitive intuition that senses trouble with someone ahead of time only needs to be channeled toward thinking in terms of solutions. It takes less energy to confront a problem if someone is willing to work with you on solving it. Running away is not the same as taking a pause to gather your thoughts. Your relationships get empowered when teaming up with a partner to deal with an issue. The more you practice doing this, the less likelihood there is of this past life shadow showing its face. You are stronger than you might realize. As you learn to engage assertively in handling challenges as they arise, this past life pattern stays away.

The Sounds of Silence pattern indicates a quietness that comes naturally to Pisces more than many of the other astrological signs. Taking the initiative to speak up and be present when requested by others prevents this pattern from occurring. It is fine to need time alone to gather your thoughts and recharge your brain. Finding that balance between visibility and taking time alone keeps this past life shadow force from making an entrance into this lifetime. It might take a conscious effort to realize you need to communicate your ideas. This pattern may not be so obvious to your conscious mind in your everyday interactions with people. With practice it will be an automatic response to be an active partner in a relationship. It builds trust when you show you are listening by speaking your thoughts openly to someone.

The Paradise Lost pattern is easier to let go of when you focus more on being positive. It is the sure road to finding harmony with someone. Learning to live with the ups and downs in a relationship is accepting the reality that there are no perfect people. Supporting the goals of individuals you care about sends this pattern away from you. Being a cheerleader brings out the best in others. This does not mean that you will like everything about someone. But the happiness you long for with a lover has a much better chance of happening when you perceive a person's good attributes. The bridge to attracting fulfillment in a relationship is truly believing in a person. Positive energy shows you appreciate those you want to keep close and proves you believe in them.

You can liberate yourself from the Coloring the Truth pattern when you communicate with an honest representation of yourself. Instead of trying to manipulate situations, you will find it less stressful to work toward win-win results with people. The big payoff is you can have a relationship based on trust. The love you want to receive is readily available when you stay away from only telling people what you imagine they want to hear. Letting someone into your feelings opens the door to a harmonious intimacy. It takes much less energy to be open about true perceptions rather than trying to conceal them. This past life tendency is less problematic when you show you are bringing your most authentic game into a relationship.

The Comparison Shopping pattern can be lessened in its influence if you come to grips with the reality that the past does not need to rule the present. Learning what you liked and learned from past relationships, whether from a past incarnation or the current one, is valuable. There is an excellent possibility that in meeting someone new it will be a better match for where you have evolved to in the current life. You could be in denial about what was not so good in a past relationship, only longing for what you liked about a person. Setting yourself free to explore the harmony you can create with a new love can liberate you from this past life shadow.

The My Truth Is the Truth pattern needs you not to lose sight that the opinions and ideas of others matter. Everyone wants to feel valued. Think in terms of inclusion and this past life nemesis will stay away. It is easy for emotions to tell your mind that you have the best possible solution to a problem. Let the wonderful adaptability of your Pisces sign remind you that listening to input from people you love is a great wisdom. You probably will need to slow down long enough to listen to your closest allies before running with a plan. Remember there are many paths to the truth, even though you could be convinced your own thoughts are the best. Stay away from being critical of those trying to support your goals with their own insights. The love and harmony you cherish stays strong when you open your mind to new ideas from those you trust.

The Pisces Reward from Solving Karmic Patterns

You are fortunate to be born a Pisces with a strong intuition. It gives you the capacity to believe that you can find your way to rise above the challenge presented by any karmic pattern. It takes determination and patience to face a past life pattern. The first awareness of a past life shadow is the beginning of a magical journey to self-discovery. Your emotions as a water sign are likely intense at times. When you step back and don't judge yourself, the insights into healing a past life energy are very possible.

If you did see yourself in any of the past life patterns discussed, don't let it make you feel overly anxious. Remember this is a learning experience without a deadline to meet. Go at your own pace. If you feel like you are taking one step forward and then are backtracking, that is okay. The main thing is to keep moving forward on your evolving journey.

There is a big payoff in dealing with a past life influence. Your relationships are easier to enjoy. Your way of relating gains a greater flow of harmony. The love you came into this life unfolds in ways you may never have imagined. You will be better equipped to give more generously and to receive with an open heart.

Pisces the Innocent Journal Prompts

1. How do you feel when you see the Pisces image?
2. What Pisces archetype traits do you resonate most with?
3. In what ways do you withdraw and escape from the world?
4. What are your artistic and creative talents?
5. Are you too trusting?
6. How can you develop stronger boundaries?
7. What past life patterns have you experienced?

Conclusion

Carmen and Bernie want to thank you, the reader, for joining us on a journey in this book. When you think about it, our lives are fascinating adventures. Whatever your Sun sign is, the universe will send you those synchronistic experiences that will guide you toward those paths that offer new insights. It only takes our openness to allow this to occur.

Each of us is a mixture of the twelve astrological signs. Life is a twelve-step process. It is likely there will be chapters in this book that call to you to read them alongside your own Sun sign chapter. The magic of astrology is that it is a language that helps us determine why we have incarnated. It reveals our current life tendencies to seek love, inner peace and to find a true purpose.

Don't be disturbed by the past life patterns described in this book. None of us are perfect. If you came across a pattern in your Sun sign chapter that resonates with you, it is possible to transform this energy into positive expression. Our current life is an opportunity to heal past life tendencies.

A powerful message in this book is to trust your sixth sense intuition. Your intuition is the lighthouse that, during challenging times, will show you paths in to the light of clarity. Your intuition is a powerful, empowering force that is a true ally.

It is an absolute joy for Carmen and Bernie to share *Astrology's Zodiac Archetypes* with the world! Thank you for allowing us to share the book with you!

O-BOOKS

SPIRITUALITY

O is a symbol of the world, of oneness and unity; this eye
represents knowledge and insight. We publish titles on
general spirituality and living a spiritual life. We aim to
inform and help you on your own journey in this life.
If you have enjoyed this book, why not tell other readers
by posting a review on your preferred book site?

Recent Bestsellers from O-Books Are:

Heart of Tantric Sex
Diana Richardson
Revealing Eastern secrets of deep love and
intimacy to Western couples.
Paperback: 978-1-90381-637-0 ebook: 978-1-84694-637-0

Crystal Prescriptions
The A-Z guide to over 1,200 symptoms and their healing
crystals
Judy Hall
The first in the popular series of eight books, this handy
little guide is packed as tight as a pill bottle with
crystal remedies for ailments.
Paperback: 978-1-90504-740-6 ebook: 978-1-84694-629-5

Naked in the Now
Marijke McCandless
What if getting present was less like work and more like being seduced by a lover?
Paperback: 978-1-80341-567-3 ebook: 978-1-80341-574-1

Crystal Creed
Jamie Inglett
A beginner's guide to learning the sacred healing powers of crystals.
Paperback: 978-1-80341-438-6 ebook: 978-1-80341-439-3

Revealing Light
Maryann Weston
YouTube psychic-astrologer Maryann Weston, from Revealing Light, shares her spiritual evolution after cancer had activated dormant psychic gifts, revealing a new purpose...
Paperback: 978-1-80341-730-1 ebook: 978-1-80341-738-7

Temple of Love
Natalie Glebova
The secret to true love is closer than you think.
Paperback: 978-1-80341-784-4 ebook: 978-1-80341-810-0

Breath for Health
A Mindful Way to Restore Your Natural Breathing Cycle
Michael D Hutchinson
Discover the secrets hidden in yoga and modern physiology — and restore your natural, healthy, confident way of breathing in just 10 minutes a day.
Paperback: 978-1-80341-440-9 ebook: 978-1-80341-441-6

Readers of ebooks can buy or view any of these
bestsellers by clicking on the live link in the title.
Most titles are published in paperback and as an ebook.
Paperbacks are available in traditional bookshops.
Both print and ebook formats are available online.

Find more titles and sign up to our readers' newsletter at
www.o-books.com

Follow O-Books on Facebook at **O-Books**

You Tube

For video content, author interviews, and more, please subscribe to our YouTube channel:

O-BOOKS Publishing

Follow us on social media for book news, promotions, and more:

Facebook: O-Books

Instagram: @o_books_mbs

X: @obooks

Tik Tok: @ObooksMBS

www.o-books.com